NETWORK MARKETING

The Daily Express Guides

The Daily Express and Kogan Page have joined forces to publish a series of practical guides offering no-nonsense advice on a wide range of financial, legal and business topics.

Whether you want to manage your money better, make more money, get a new business idea off the ground – and make sure it's legal – there's a Daily Express Guide for you.

Titles published so far are:

Be Your Own Boss!
How to Set Up a Successful Small Business
David Mc Mullan

How to Cut Your Tax Bill Without Breaking the Law
Grant Thornton, Chartered Accountants

How to Sell More!
A Guide for Small Business
Neil Johnson

Great Ideas for Making Money
Niki Chesworth

Readymade Business Letters That Get Results
Jim Douglas

You and the Law
A Simple Guide to All Your Legal Problems
Susan Singleton

Your Money
How to Make the Most of it
Niki Chesworth

Available from all good bookshops, or to obtain further information please contact the publishers at the address below:

Kogan Page Ltd
120 Pentonville Road
London N1 9JN
Tel: 071-278 0433
Fax: 071-837 6348

Daily Express

NETWORK MARKETING
An Introductory Guide

DAVID BARBER

KOGAN
PAGE

First published in 1994

Kogan Page Limited
120 Pentonville Road
London N1 9JN

British Library Cataloguing in Publication Data

A CIP record for this book is available from the British Library.

ISBN 0 7494 1331 X

Typeset by Books Unlimited (Nottm), Rainworth, NG21 0EJ

Printed and bound in Great Britain by Clays Ltd, St Ives plc

Contents

Preface

Network marketing is a form of distribution and sales still not well understood in this country; it is too new and too divergent in approach from traditional business attitudes to have been properly investigated by the business community, and people only really see it in its proper context if they happen to come into contact with a successful practitioner – that, in itself, being a form of networking.

The purpose of this book is to:

- discover what network marketing actually is;
- uncover some popular misconceptions: in other words, what it is *not*;
- see if we can help you to decide whether or not network marketing is something you should be involved in;
- and, if you do decide to become involved, show you how to choose a reputable company.

Like most businesses, network marketing has its own trade jargon and definitions. Most of the terms will become clear to you as you read on. If they do not, you will find a glossary in Chapter 10.

As in any business, companies vary in the way in which they apply the concept and in their reward structure. If you were lent this book by an independent distributor, he or she will give you the information you need. If not, you should contact any company you are interested in directly. (I will show you how to find likely companies in Chapter 5.)

Warning

Network marketing is a very strong concept where the company, the product and the distributor come together in the right way. If you are considering becoming a distributor, there are, however, companies which are best avoided. Also, unethical distributors can exist in even the best companies and you should avoid being sponsored by one of these. It is not difficult to choose an ethical company and a good sponsor provided you use caution, common sense and follow the guidelines in this book. You should also check with the Direct Selling Association (DSA), 29 Floral Street, London WC2E 9DP (phone 071-497 1234) who will send you a free DSA/DTI advice sheet and information pack. However, the DSA can only promote its members, so do not dismiss a company simply because it is a non-member: some opportunities as good do exist outside.

The Department of Trade and Industry has issued a useful free booklet on the industry. You can get this from either your local DTI office (the address will be in your Yellow Pages under 'Government Offices') or the Direct Selling Association.

Network marketing started in the United States of America and is now spreading throughout Europe. It offers a business opportunity for people with no commercial background provided they choose a company wisely and take advantage of the training and advice available. This book spells out the perks and the pitfalls.

1
What is network marketing?

Network marketing is one the 'chains of distribution'. These are the different ways in which a supplier or manufacturer can get his product from his premises or factory gate to the end-consumer, in other words, you or I buying it for our own use.

What are the main chains of distribution?

1. *Traditional retailing*. This is where the product goes from the supplier, perhaps through one or more distributors, to a wholesaler and then to a retailer. You or I then buy that product from the retailer.
2. *Mail order*. Selling to the end-consumer by the use of leaflets, catalogues or media advertising and without the intervention of a salesperson or agent.
3. *Direct selling*. This is selling to end-consumers in their homes or at their places of work. The three main ways of doing this are using:

- direct salespeople or catalogue agents;
- party plan;
- network marketing, which uses independent distributors.

You can see from this that network marketing is a branch of direct selling.

How does network marketing differ from multi-level marketing?

Network marketing is a form of multi-level marketing (MLM) which is the generic or catch-all name for any form of business designed to grow through levels or lines being formed by self-employed, independent people creating their own businesses by recruiting or 'sponsoring' others into their organisation, rather than the company doing its own recruiting.

The line between network marketing and MLM is not, at the time of writing, fully defined. Some companies, writers and trainers use network marketing interchangeably with MLM; others, such as myself, increasingly use the expression for the one ethical form of MLM which has been proved to provide the potential for a professional and long-term career, and this custom appears to be gathering momentum. To save confusion, all you need to do is understand that different companies use the expression differently.

Multi-level marketing is fully described by Peter Clothier, a former trading standards inspector, in his book, *Multi-level Marketing* (Kogan Page, 2nd edition, 1992).

How does network marketing differ from traditional business?

Traditional companies employ salespeople, or use self-employed agents or distributors to generate sales, each in a strictly defined local area. If you were a traditional salesperson, agent or distributor, your area would be yours alone and other people would not normally be allowed to sell in it. The opposite is also true; you would not be allowed to sell in another salesperson's area, either.

But a company using network marketing as its chain of distribution gives individuals the right to handle its products by setting up their own businesses with only national (or, if the company has become international, then international) geographic boundaries. The distributors then expand their businesses by introducing or sponsoring other people into the network to do the same, irrespective of where they are in the country. They in turn expand their businesses by sponsoring others, and so on.

Another major difference between network marketing and traditional retailing is in the much simpler distribution system used by network marketing. You can see this from the following chart:

Few of the headings shown in figure 1.1 under traditional retailing are cost centres which occur in network marketing with the exception of a much lower level of promotion.

Typically, the costs incurred in traditional retailing account for between 60 and 90 per cent of the retail or selling price a product, excluding VAT. By saving most of these costs, the supplier can offer discounts to distributors on orders placed by them, and commission or royalty on orders placed by the distributors they themselves have sponsored into the network.

How important is network marketing?

Network marketing, then known only as multi-level marketing, was established in the early 1940s. Since then, it has become a fast-expanding part of the American business scene – so much so, indeed, that it is estimated that there is an independent distributor in one in ten North American homes. The vast majority are part time. The American Direct Selling Association estimates that its 150 members moved $12 billion-worth of goods in 1992,

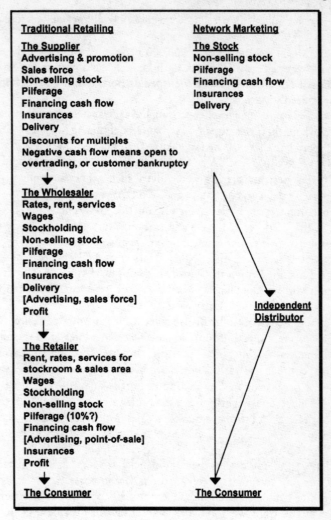

Figure 1.1 *A comparison between cost centres in traditional retailing and network marketing*

and increased sales by 8.8 per cent in 1993. The number of people involved increased from 3.6 million in 1987 to over 5 million in 1992.

Although the concept is considered a new one in the UK, there are already two British household names involved – the famous Kleeneze and Dorling Kindersley (or DK) Family Library. The latter is one of the UK's highest-profile publishers and you will see large ranges of their titles in bookshops, at motorway service stations, and so on. The level of UK business is surprising: the latest available figures (1992) were £189 million – an increase of 53.6 per cent over the previous two-year period, in a recession! The *Observer* (February 1992) estimated that 500,000 people, a population the size of Liverpool, were already involved: again, largely on a part-time basis. That represents about 1½ per cent of the working population. Yet network marketing has hardly started here!

Statistics abound. The market-leading life assurance company in the USA is a network marketing company. Herbalife, specialising in dietary products, has a 10 per cent share of the large Australian market. Network marketing companies lead the UK, USA and world markets in such diverse fields as car immobilisers, personal alarms, water filters, dietary and slimming products, car fuel-saving devices, cosmetics, and so on. Amway has the biggest single-location computer in North America, outside the Pentagon. The largest buyers in the world of aloe vera and carbon filters are Forever Living and NSA respectively. The companies with an established track record over years include: Amway, Herbalife, NSA, Mary Kay, Kleeneze, Cabouchon, Nature's Sunshine Products. Outside network marketing, the direct selling companies you are most likely to have heard of are Avon, Tupperware, Ann Summers, Pippa Dee and Bettawear.

The experience of both the British and the North American Direct Selling Associations is that, as a group, direct selling companies (and this includes network marketing companies) perform far better through recessions than traditional companies. Indeed, while companies in most market sectors (including the professions) show a drop in profits or turnover, direct selling companies have consistently increased both turnover and profits through recession. The DSA estimates that total sales in the UK (both for members and non-members involved in direct selling) increased from £798.8 million in 1991 to £831.7 million in 1992, having risen from £507 million in 1987; these figures exclude direct sales of financial services, double glazing and other home improvements involving direct labour costs.

Where the company, the product and the independent distributor come together in the right way, network marketing can provide a genuine and viable alternative to any other form of occupation, profession, career or business.

2

How is the money earned?

There are three ways of earning income from network marketing:

1. Retailing
2. Wholesaling
3. Royalty (or commission).

Retailing

The distributor buys the products at a wholesale price and sells them at a retail price. The difference is the retail margin or retail profit. A distributor's main source of customers is going to be his warm market (friends, relations, neighbours and acquaintances) and his secondary warm market (people recommended to him by his warm market). In addition to this, some companies, but not all, will also let distributors sell to their cold market (people not personally known to them) through advertising, mail order or door-to-door selling. If you are attached to a catalogue company, some, but again not all, will let you sell to your cold market by delivering catalogues door to door.

Wholesaling

This is income made from a wholesale discount earned by supplying other distributors in the same group. At the bottom position of the marketing plan, described on page 90, there is usually no wholesale discount but, as distributors go up the ladder, the wholesale discount to which they are entitled increases. The distributor gets the wholesale discount even though the company delivers direct to his people, so he may not even have to handle the product. This also means that, as he promotes himself up the marketing plan, he will also make more money out of his personal retail sales because he adds his wholesale discount to the retail profit.

Royalty

This is a percentage commission paid on all the sales through a distributor's group, down a certain number of levels or 'generations' (see page 86-88). The reason why royalty is not paid throughout all a distributor's business, irrespective of the number of levels, is because eventually the total being paid out in royalties would be more than the retail price of the product.

The distributor's actual income is derived from two activities: retailing and sponsoring. I hasten to add that no good network marketing company actually pays anything for sponsoring. But, if the intention is to build a reasonable business, sponsoring will be the major source of income, albeit indirectly, because the people a distributor brings in will also retail product and he will earn from what they retail. There is a limit to how much retailing one person can physically do on their own, so the way to earn more than this limit is to recruit more people to help move more product and then to earn from their efforts.

What does a distributor need to know?

Most people would expect a change of career to involve not only considerable retraining but also a need to gather broad practical experience before they could even start to become successful. However, the knowledge required to be a successful independent distributor is simple, and distributors acquire it while actually doing business and earning. The majority do not to come from a sales background and would not go into another branch of the sales profession if they left network marketing.

Distributors do not need to have any previous business, sales or even work experience. This is because the concept is based on three remarkably simple ideas which are easily learnt:

1. Independent distributors find a product they can identify with and show it to people they know – friends, relations, neighbours and acquaintances or to people introduced by them.
2. With the help of people already experienced in the business, distributors show a simple business opportunity to friends, relations, neighbours and acquaintances or to people introduced by them.
3. In distributors' own time, and as their confidence, knowledge and experience grow, in a simple way, they teach people coming into the business to do the same thing.

Getting started

The vast majority of people who go into network marketing have never been in sales before and the prospect of selling or retailing can frighten them. It need not do so because the way to succeed is not for a distributor to charge off 'door-knocking' or pinning friends to the wall until they buy.

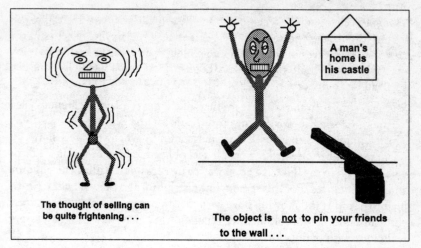

The thought of selling can be quite frightening . . .

The object is <u>not</u> to pin your friends to the wall . . .

A man's home is his castle

The aim of network marketing is to have more friends, not fewer! Retailing is very much easier than that. There are in fact three stages, of which the first is very simple.

- Exposing and supplying
- Showing
- Selling.

Exposing and supplying means three simple steps:

1. Have the product available for people to see
2. Make people aware that you have it
3. Let them know that you can supply it.

Constantly using the product yourself and letting other people see that you do is how you carry out steps 1 and 2. This is the reason for the rule in network marketing: 'Distributors must themselves be users of the product', or to put it another way, 'Distributors must be their own best customers.'

The other way of exposing and supplying is to let the product do its own selling by leaving it with the customer to have a look at and offering to include it on the next order if they would like to buy it. If the product is left free of charge for the customer to try, this is called 'puppy dog' selling on the theory that if you leave a puppy dog on trial with a person, they won't want to give it back.

Exposing and supplying is called 'passive' selling and, unless a distributor is experienced in sales or confident of his ability, it is where he should start.

Showing is changing the technique from 'passive' to 'positive'. Instead of just leaving the product to sell itself, the distributor explains its benefits to the customer but leaves the customer completely open to make their own mind up. An easy way to do this is to say, 'Let me know if you would like one and I will add it to my order.'

Selling is similar to showing except that it includes the sales technique called 'closing'. Closing means making it difficult for the customer to say 'No'. This technique has to be used extremely carefully when you are selling to a warm market because making people feel obliged to buy, or making it difficult for them to say 'No', is a good way to lose friends, relations, neighbours and acquaintances. For this reason, few distributors go that far and the great majority stop at the showing stage with their warm market although, if their company does allow cold market retailing, they may well use the closing technique with their cold market.

If a product is suitable for party plan selling or catalogue drops, retailing is even easier, because it is possible for distributors to sponsor party planners or catalogue agents to do the retailing for them. Party plan selling takes place in someone's home, to which guests are invited to inspect stock and place orders.

To start with, most income is likely to come from retailing and/or some wholesale discounts. As the business grows and a distributor progresses up the marketing plan, wholesale discounts will take over as the main source of income and royalties will start to come in. Even though they will be a tiny percentage compared with retail margins and wholesale discounts, royalties become the major source of income once the big business-builder stage is reached. So, although royalties are the smallest percentage figure in a bonus structure, they are easily the most significant.

Introducing your product or the business opportunity to friends and relatives.

Some people have difficulty with this, either through embarrassment or through inexperience. If you lose friends, you have shown them the product or the business incorrectly, because you have put them under pressure. If you make sure you never get beyond 'exposing' or 'showing' you will not lose friends. Making people aware of what you have and showing it to them never loses friendships; it is doing it in a way which makes them feel beholden to you, embarrassed or guilty if they do not help you by buying, which causes the problem. You will actually strengthen your friendship if they buy a product from you which gives them some benefit or if they come into your business and do well. Remember the rule: if you would not buy the product yourself, if it is not good enough to show to friends, then you should not be handling it.

But, if it is that good, do not fall into the trap of selling to people you know at cost! This is your business. The product should be good enough to warrant the full price and, if they do not buy it from you, they would have to pay the full price elsewhere. A good friend or relative will respect that if you explain it to them.

Who gets involved?

The answer is – anyone and everyone! This sounds like a flippant answer but in fact the business, by its very nature, crosses all the boundaries of society, whether they be of background, education, age, sex, race, colour, previous experience, wealth or lack of it.

The basic reason why most people, whoever they are and whatever their situation in life, become involved in network marketing is because they are seeking to improve their lives.

Broadly speaking, the business might appeal to people who:

1. Are happy with their present method of earning a living but are looking for a supplementary income to help with holidays, a new car, the mortgage, school fees, a hobby, and so on.
2. Are trying to take control of their life, perhaps by getting out of serious financial difficulties or work-related problems, or seeking to realise their ambitions.
3. Are high-flyers who want to devote time and effort to their ambitions and who are looking for the greatest income return or the fastest career progression in return for their commitment.
4. Want to earn what they are worth rather than what someone chooses to pay them.
5. Prefer to be promoted on results rather than rely on the judgement of superiors. Just as in normal business, there is a 'ladder' system of promotion, with clearly defined job titles and extra benefits as you go up. But, in network marketing, you are not promoted by someone above you and only if there happens to be a vacancy; you promote yourself as your business grows. There is no one to hold you back.
6. Want to enjoy a money-making social life and a feeling of belonging through network marketing.
7. Are looking for a work environment where they can increase their self-confidence, learn to communicate better, feel a greater appreciation for

their efforts, generally get more for themselves out of life, or learn to make the maximum use of themselves and their talents.

8. Are attracted by one of the maxims of network marketing: 'You can only succeed by helping other people to succeed.'

Some part-time distributors join up specifically to contribute part or all of their income to favourite charitable causes. For people like nurses, social workers or teachers, it allows them to carry on their socially valuable, but badly paid, jobs without sacrificing their lifestyle. Ministers of religion use the concept to fund their religious activities. Charities on occasion use MLM techniques to raise funds.

Examples of people who are commonly seen in network marketing

1. People who are looking for a part-time income or an additional profit centre; or who are perhaps unable (maybe for family or health reasons) to take on full-time employment.
2. Entrepreneurs or self-employed people.
3. Unqualified manual workers or shop-workers; people whose jobs are redundant or who are unemployed; people who feel held back by discrimination on the grounds of race or colour, age, sex, education, experience, social background or medical condition.
4. Professional people or people from a vocational or caring background.
5. Executives, managers or directors; chairpersons of corporations; or people aspiring to these positions.

One of the more interesting ways in which people are introduced to network marketing is when an accountant, banker or lawyer is asked by a client to check the business out for them; this has frequently resulted in the professional adviser also coming into the business.

There is no room for discrimination in this business for one very good reason: it would actually limit a distributor's earning capacity. Even if a distributor were to be prejudiced against one sector of society and therefore decided not to invite those people to come into his business, he would have no control over those brought in by other distributors in his group. Groups naturally become cosmopolitan very quickly.

The fact that network marketing puts a financial penalty on prejudice makes it unique in business, commercial, professional and even religious circles.

The system of network marketing provides a business opportunity for people from almost any background; it is easier to categorise people to whom network marketing might appeal more by what they want from the business than by their character, personality, social background or experience. Often they are seeking to solve the ATAC equation:

Abundant Time, Abundant Cash =
Abundant Time to do the things they want to do and Abundant Cash to do them with.

The ATAC equation varies enormously from person to person: a hermit needs very little cash and has plenty of time, but a pleasure-seeking tycoon is going to have great difficulty in finding the time for both work and play and is going to need mountains of cash to indulge his lifestyle! It follows from this that the more ambitious you are or the more you want for your family, the harder it will be to solve your ATAC equation.

Earning income is not the only reason to do network marketing, though it may be possible to earn large sums of money; many distributors feel that this is the least of what it has to offer because there are many other benefits in the system and we shall have a closer look at these in Chapter 4.

3

How does the system work?

The traditional retailing system consists of wholesalers and retailers. In network marketing, these are replaced by independent distributors (IDs) who do the distribution and selling.

Although some companies accept orders from, and make deliveries to, distributors direct from the start, in most companies orders are placed with the person who introduced the distributor to the network (who is known as his *sponsor*) until he is accepted by the company on a direct basis. Cash with order is the general rule.

Whereas the traditional business area is geographic, the network marketing 'area' is a person's so-called *warm market*: the people they know (friends, relations and acquaintances), irrespective of where those people live. In practice, even people living next door to one another rarely have the same warm market. Far from local independent distributors seeing one another as competitors, which is precisely what would happen in traditional business if you were to have salespeople, agents or distributors without clearly defined local areas, local network marketeers do the complete opposite and band together as far as possible in order to help one another. This aspect of the concept can surprise those who have been affected by the in-fighting and company politics which can occur in corporate business; true network marketeers are much more likely to display a spontaneous willingness to help one another.

The big advantage of the sponsoring system is that, by introducing just a few people and everyone else doing the same thing, a distributor can quite quickly finish up with a large network. In fact, he could build up his sales operation far more quickly than is possible in a traditional business and 'cash in' on John Paul Getty's statement that he would rather earn from 1 per cent of 100 people's efforts than from 100 per cent of his own. In fact, in network marketing, the figure is nearer 3 – 6 per cent of as many *effective* people as the distributor has in his business.

So how does this work? Any distributor can sponsor as many or as few people as he likes but let's say, to keep it simple, that he sponsors only five people and everyone he brings in decides to do the same. His business would grow as follows:

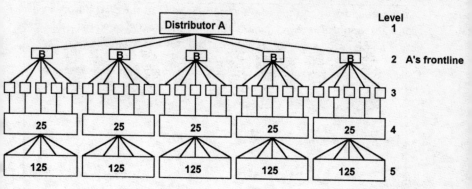

Figure 3.1 *This is an example of distributor's downline based on five introductions per person, and supposing each one stays in the network*

- On level 1 is distributor A.
- Level 2 has five people on it – the people A has sponsored who are known as his frontline.
- His frontline each bring in five distributors and this gives him 25 people on level 3. Each group of five forms the frontline of their sponsor.
- The 25 distributors on level 3 each bring in five people and this gives distributor A 125 people on level 4.
- The 125 distributors on level 4 each bring in five people and that gives him 625 people on level 5.

Add all the levels together and, although A brought in only five people (and no one else has done more), he now has 781 people (including himself) in his business. One feature to note is that his fifth level has more people on it than the total of all the other levels added together. This means that, once he has built his fifth level, his income should double provided the average orders per distributor remain the same and the entire downline stays in the network. If there is an 80 per cent drop-out rate, the downline looks like the example in Figure 3.2.

But if I am only sponsoring one person a month . . . what do I do for the rest of the month?

This form of growth is called either a *geometric equation* or an *exponential curve* and it is one of the most important things you need to understand about network marketing because it is at the core of the system. Let me give you an example of how it works.

If A sponsors only one person a month and if all the distributors in his group also sponsor one person a month, his business growth over the first year is going to look like this if everyone stays in the network:

Table 3.1 *Business growth based on each distributor introducing one new one each monthly*

Month	IDs at start of month		New IDs		Network total
1	A	+	1	=	2
2	2	+	2	=	4
3	4	+	4	=	8
4	8	+	8	=	16
5	16	+	16	=	32
6	32	+	32	=	64
7	64	+	64	=	128
8	128	+	128	=	256
8	256	+	256	=	512
10	512	+	512	=	1024
11	1024	+	1024	=	2048
12	2048	+	2048	=	4096

The important things to stress about this growth are:

- A has sponsored only 12 people (and no one else has sponsored more than 11) and no one has sponsored more than one a month.
- Nothing much happens until the tenth month, then it explodes!

Even if you were to suffer a drop-out rate of 90 per cent, you would have a network 400 strong at the end of a year.

If you apply the same rules to the business growth in fives which we gave as an example in Figure 3.1, you will see:

- No one, including A, has sponsored more than five people.
- Nothing much happens until the fifth level, then it explodes!

It is important to realise that the geometric equation needs time to grow. Many people give up after three months because they 'only' have eight people in their business. Look at that chart again: eight people after three months puts them right on course for 4096 after 12 months. Another critical time for drop-outs is after six months because they 'only' have 64 people in their business. Look again: they too are on course for 4096 after 12 months.

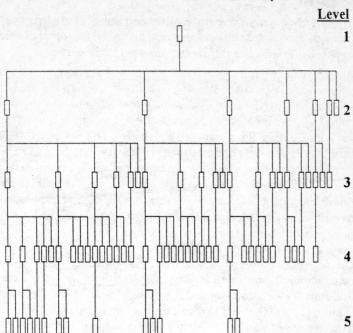

Level

1

2

3

4

5

Figure 3.2 *A network of 781 people, of whom only 10 per cent are active. As people drop out, others move up from the lower levels*

In fact, if everyone in A's group sponsors an average of only one person every five months, he will still be on course for a business of 4096 after five years.

One word of warning: *the figures are not as simple to achieve as they seem.* When we say sponsor one person a month, what we mean is one person a month who will stick at it and will themselves continue to sponsor one good person a month who will do the same thing. Second, it is no good just sponsoring even a good person a month and letting them get on with it; you need to train, lead and motivate them. So, to answer the cartoon character who asks, 'What do I do for the rest of the month?', you work with the people who have come into your business, helping them to succeed.

If you do not keep your network motivated to continue, you could suffer heavy drop-out, as shown in Figure 3.2.

Also, growth rates flatten out dramatically of their own accord after a while but the essential philosophy behind the theory is valid. It is important to give the geometric equation time to work. An enormous number of distributors drop out when they are actually on course for a large business but do not realise it.

With all this sponsoring going on, who is doing the selling?

Although all distributors seem to put a great deal of effort behind sponsoring, there often seems to be almost no emphasis on selling and surely, unless people sell product, a lot of product, no one is going to earn anything, and certainly not the five-figure incomes per month which are bandied about.

Let's look at that chart on page 25 again. If all A's 780 people were part time and averaging only one sale a week, each worth, let's say, £50 per sale, this could (depending on which programme A is in) earn him the staggering figure of £5000 a month. Based on these figures, halving the sales to only two a month per distributor would still earn A £30,000 a year. So one of the secrets of network marketing is that it is a lot of people doing a little bit, not, as in normal business, a few superstars doing a lot.

Look at Figure 3.3 opposite

Let me explain this chart. 'D' stands for distributor and the number stands for the number of distributors along that level. For instance, A has three distributors on his second level (2D plus distributor B) and six on his third (3D plus 2D plus C). C has 15 distributors on his fourth level (6D plus 9D).

You also need to understand that all companies only pay you down a set number of levels. In this case, we have assumed that the company pays its distributors on four levels and so, to avoid confusion, we have stopped each of the distributors A to D at their fourth levels.

Again to simplify matters, we have chosen to highlight the businesses of just four distributors: A to D. As you can see, A sponsored B, who sponsored C, who sponsored D.

Remember that you promote yourself by the size of business you have, and answer this question: which of the distributors has promoted himself past A by building a bigger business than A – is it B, C or D? The answer is: all of them. B's business has 24 distributors (including himself), C has 25 and D has 28. A, however, has only 23 distributors.

So, whereas in traditional business the hierarchy would go exactly as in Figure 3.3 and B, C and D would not be able to get the promotion they deserved, the network marketing system has allowed each person to find his own level – in this case exactly reversing the traditional hierarchy.

Levels

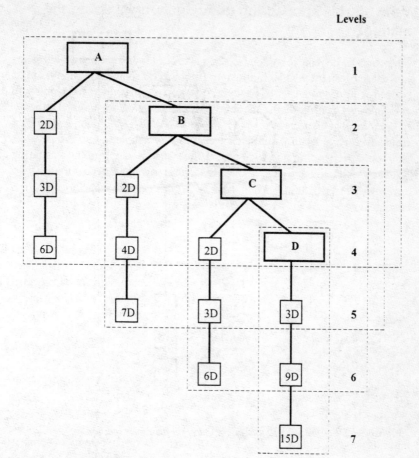

Figure 3.3 *Specimen network*

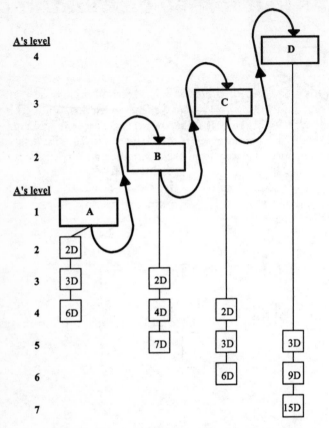

Figure 3.4 *Distributors can build bigger networks than their sponsor*

Figure 3.4 is exactly the same business as A's in figure 3.3, but this time it has been rewritten to show the flexibility of his network marketing business:

A will be delighted that he has four downline distributors who have built bigger businesses than he has, because he earns royalties off his downlines and the bigger the businesses they build, the more he will earn.

If you want to build a big business, this chart also shows you that the secret is to find as many people as possible who are actually better than you at network marketing because the better they are, the more you will earn. That is somewhat different from traditional business, where superiors may restrict or hold back employees who are better than they are.

4

What's in it for the distributors?

Distributors join looking for either a low-level commitment or a high-level commitment, or something in between. Generally speaking, someone looking for a low-level commitment is a part-timer and someone looking for a medium to high-level commitment is a full-timer. Having said that, some distributors can earn as much from their part-time activity as from their full-time occupation.

Many people begin on a part-time basis with the intention of building their network marketing business into a full-time career. If this is your intention, it is wise not to go full time too soon; wait until you can afford to do this financially.

What do part-timers look for?

1. *Potentially high earnings for part-timers*. The earnings can be high compared with most part-time jobs which, by their very nature, can be menial or undemanding and therefore attract low rates of pay. Highly paid, part-time occupations tend to be in the traditional sales field and this is not an option which the majority of distributors would consider. However, network marketing deserves a close look from salespeople who could earn considerably more from a network marketed product than from the same product being sold on commission.

2. *The social life*. This is a pleasant side benefit. There is spontaneous and immediate acceptance of new people. Most enjoy the quickly made but lasting friendships which are forged among distributors, and this stems partly from the fact that everyone enjoys what they are doing and partly because, perhaps for the first time in their lives, people feel free to do what they want to do and be who they want to be. Whether they are in the same company or not, distributors enjoy the camaraderie found in any club or organisation.

3. *Complete flexibility of hours*. You work when you want to, not when someone else is expecting you to. In many part-time jobs, you are required to fit in with certain hours, and trying to change those hours can be at worst frowned upon and at best inconvenient in that you may have to find someone else to cover for you or swop rotas. Network marketing is totally flexible; for instance, a mother can vary her work pattern

according to whether it is term time or school holidays; a business person, who is using his network marketing business as an additional profit-centre, can shelve it when his core business is busy and use the extra time profitably when his core business is slack.

During a recession people from all professions can use their periods of enforced idleness to good effect by networking, knowing that, once things get better in their 'day job', they can cut back on their network marketing businesses to compensate.

What advantages are there for full-timers or career network marketeers?

1. *A high-level business with a minimal investment.* The costs of getting involved are minimal and we will come back to this in more detail on page 64. However, no matter how big your business becomes, the only stock you will need could comfortably be kept under your stairs or in an out-of-the-way corner.

2. *There is minimal risk on stock purchase.* We will cover this in detail later, but you will find that you have a minimum legal 90 per cent buy-back clause in your contract. In addition, you cannot be required to buy stock until you have already pre-sold it.

3. *The cash flow is positive.* Normal business operates on what is called **negative cash flow**. This means (unless you are running a retail shop) that you are paid only after delivery of an order to your customer. People who supply shops find that retailers can take on average 60 days to pay their bills. In some industries, even that is fast payment. This can cause a situation called **overtrading** in which a company finds that it has not got enough ready cash to pay its bills, even though it has more than enough money to cover them owed to it by its customers. It is one of the biggest criticisms of our present banking system that a company with a huge 'paper' profit can get into trouble by being too successful. But the sad fact is that overtrading is a major cause of bankruptcy.

   Operating with negative cash flow (i.e. offering credit) means that, in general, your customers always owe you money. This means that another major cause of company failure is the bankruptcy of a major customer.

   The opposite of negative cash flow is **positive cash flow**. In simple terms, positive cash flow means that everything is cash with order. In other words, customers pay the distributor cash with order and the distributor pays the company cash with order. This is a protection against both overtrading and customer bankruptcy (if customers do not owe money to you or distributors in your group, their bankruptcy or non-payment cannot put you or any of your people at risk).

But cash with order throughout the system has another advantage. Network marketing allows distributors in serious financial difficulty to set up a business with virtually no capital; if the system was based on credit, companies would have to run credit checks which would automatically disbar them.

4. *There is an exceptional earning potential*. Unlike normal business, there is theoretically no limit to earnings. This is proved by the high earnings which some distributors achieve.

5. *The overheads are minimal*. No matter how big you get, you do not need:

- a warehouse
- offices
- staff
- bank borrowings.

6. *Self-promotion is based entirely on results*. You cannot be demoted! Each promotion is permanent. Suppose you start as a part-timer when your main job or business is slack. You get a couple of promotions and then your full-time occupation suddenly demands all your time and, for two months, you find you can spend no time at all on your network marketing business. As a result, when you come back in two months, you may well have to start again – but you will start again in the same position as you left. If you qualified for a higher buying discount before you left, you will come back at that discount level.

There are none of the barriers to promotion which you meet in traditional business, where the first hurdle is that you are likely to have to rely totally on a superior's assessment of whether you are good enough to be promoted. The second is that, even if your company does consider that you deserve promotion, they may not have a vacant position to which to promote you. This gives you the choice of either sitting around waiting for 'dead-men's shoes' or moving to a new company.

In network marketing, you can climb the 'corporate' ladder just as fast as your determination and commitment will let you, unhampered by any obstacles outside yourself.

7. *It is simple; anyone and everyone can do it*. The business allows everyone the same, equal, access to the top. Apart from making a distributor feel

good, there is a major advantage in this – it means that he can show the business to anyone without having to worry about whether or not they have the right credentials.

8. *Security*. Security means different things to different people. You may feel that security comes from having a potentially high income. Or your definition may be having a saleable asset because you can sell your network on the open market; what, for instance, is the market value of a business earning £5000 a month with no borrowings, liabilities or the millstones of premises, staff or bad debts? Or is security to you building a business which you can leave to your spouse or family if anything should happen to you? This is a business you can pass on to your heirs.

Security has latterly taken on a new meaning; no matter how good you are in your field, business or job security is now a thing of the past. The modern employment environment is no respecter of reputations; and bankruptcies, redundancies and cut-backs clear out the good with the bad, the deserving with the undeserving. So what many people now want, above all else, is work security which is not dependent on the whims of forces outside their control.

If you were a distributor and your network marketing company were to go bankrupt today, or if its product were to stop selling today, you could be up and running tomorrow in a new network. And, if you have looked after the people in your group well enough, many of them would go with you. That is the real security and one of the most telling advantages of network marketing over traditional business. The ability to be able to start up again tomorrow with a strong network of people who have moved with you, should anything go wrong with your business today, is a powerful incentive in these days of constant worry over job or business security.

9. *Freedom*. Most people in business for themselves describe their lives as a constant struggle, with personal guarantees up to the hilt, unco-operative local planners, difficulty in finding staff with a commitment to quality and productivity, and the only way to expand being to borrow yet more money from bank managers who do not understand the needs of business.

Although business people are their own bosses and many live a good life, few would consider themselves free! People who are on the corporate ladder are no different; even though they may be on high incomes, they find that the higher they go the longer hours they have to work and the less free they become. This is the complete opposite of common sense: surely the purpose of hard work and promotion is to become more free, not less so. In fact, few people feel free to live life the way they would like to.

Even lower down the ladder, there is little personal freedom to live your life the way you want to. There are few exceptions to the rule that, if you want a job, you must fit in with what the company wants in terms of both your time input and how you carry out your work.

Traditional business is so structured that those people who are not ambitious in career terms are looked down on by their more thrusting colleagues. But the network marketing system is the complete opposite: it is based on you deciding for yourself what you want, and then being shown by your more experienced uplines (the line of distributors above you) how to achieve those goals. Indeed, while attempts to get the individual to achieve more are an essential part of traditional business management, a network marketeer who tries to do the same thing will soon come unstuck. As one example of what I mean: the way to increase the sales of your group is not to motivate and train your people to sell more, it is to recruit more distributors.

10. *It is fun!* Not many people get enjoyment from their work because, as we have seen, traditional business requires them to fit in with it, rather than the other way round. The network marketing system is the complete opposite: you decide how you want to structure your life and what your business aims are and then you plan your business accordingly.

Training

The training and management aspects of network marketing are much more fulfilling than they are in traditional business. If you are a trainer or manager yourself, you will probably confirm that you spend 75 per cent of your time with your 25 per cent worst performers because that is simply how it is in traditional business. But I am also sure that you will echo the frustration of having to spend most of your time with non-achievers.

I think most of us would rather spend our time in a much more rewarding way, with people who want to make the best of themselves and learn from us, and that is precisely how successful network marketeers allocate their time.

What is required to succeed as an independent distributor?

This depends on what he wants out of the business. If he is looking only for a small extra monthly income, he may not even have to bother about the network marketing side of the business because he should be able to earn what he needs by 'retailing', selling or 'showing' the product to enough people. If the product has a high repeat value, with customers constantly re-ordering, all he needs is to build up a 'round' of customers big enough to give the target income. Other products are excellent for party plan. Yet others are ideal for both.

If the product does not have a high repeat value (or any repeat value at all), you can build up a purely sales business by using the system known as *referrals*, in which you can ask your satisfied customers to give you the names of people they know (these are known as *leads*) who might be interested in having a look at the product. So you do not need to retail your product just to people you know, you can retail to the people your customers know and to the people they know and so on, like the ripples spreading out on the surface of a pool. The easiest way to sell is by recommendation; as long as distributors always make sure that they are getting enough leads from their satisfied customers (and the better distributors look after them, the more likely they will be to want to help), they need never run out of people to sell to.

If retailing on its own will not give the desired income, distributors will have to start business-building by sponsoring and learn how to network market properly. The size of the group they need to build will be decided by how much they want to earn because, as we said earlier, you do not increase your income by trying to get the people in your group to sell more but by you, or the people in your group, sponsoring more distributors. To become successful as a business-builder, a distributor needs to look at what almost all successful network marketeers have done and copy them. So what did they do to build successful businesses?

1. *They developed a belief structure.* They acquired belief:

   - in the company
   - in the product
   - in network marketing
   - in their ability to do it.

   The need for belief is obvious: if you are going to show the business opportunity to people you know, you are not going to be successful if you do not believe in it yourself! Belief comes to some people as soon as they are shown the opportunity; to others, it comes only with time and confidence. Either way, a distributor needs to have belief so, if they do not have it, it is something they should consciously aim to build.

2. *They developed a bulldozer mentality.* This means in simple terms that, whatever obstacles they met, they kept on going. While retailing the product or building a small group may not need much determination (how much is needed depends on the product and the distributor), you must have, or develop, enough to meet your aims. But big business-building is a different proposition altogether; reaching the top in any field you care to name is definitely not a job for the faint-hearted and network marketing is no exception.

3. *They were teachable.* Although this is a simple business, it is a different way of doing things and it can be unforgiving of distributors who do not stick to a proven, simple but, it has to be stressed, narrow path.

   Many successful network marketeers will tell you that they wasted their first six months because they refused to learn. They thought that they knew better, and they tried to run their businesses in ways which countless people before had proved would not work, or they tried to cut corners. People like this can, in fact, take off like a rocket and appear to do well to start with; but the trouble with early success is that it confirms their belief that they do know best after all. They become even less teachable and, because they have not laid rock-solid foundations for their business, it may collapse a few months later like a deck of cards. Not having learnt how to run a network marketing business correctly themselves, they have been unable to teach the rest of their group how to do it right. Eventually, when they realise that people whom they considered to be less able or experienced are being more successful by sticking to the simple, proven formula, they will, if they have the right attitude, get the motivation to start again – this time, doing it right. But it is more likely that they will drop out.

4. *They did not just rely on other people, they sought out knowledge for themselves*. In other words, they took on the extra responsibility of teaching themselves. If you decide to become a distributor, treat your first six months as your apprenticeship and take for your course material the training LLAWR:

LISTEN to *successful* distributors
LISTEN to tapes on network marketing and self-development
ATTEND as many meetings and training sessions as you can
WATCH videos on network marketing and your company
READ books on network marketing and self-development

Unsuccessful distributors will rarely blame lack of success on themselves; the norm is to blame the company, the product, the concept of network marketing or their sponsor, even in cases where they patently did not do what they were advised, where the product clearly is selling and in networks where other people are succeeding. If you talk to them, you will need to take into account your personal knowledge of them and their situation, as you will not have the network marketing experience to assess the accuracy of their conclusions. But you can learn from their mistakes.

Also be critical of advice given by people who know nothing about the business, even though they might be lawyers, accountants or bankers, unless you involve them in the initial discussions. Ask around to get reliable advice. Mix with people who will genuinely support you and with success-oriented people, so that their magic can rub off on to you. You will be surprised at how willing successful network marketeers are to share their knowledge with anyone who asks them.

5. *They made themselves hungry to learn.* The more hungry you become to learn about your product, your company, how to succeed in network marketing, and self-development, the sooner you will reach the success you want.

6. *They put action into what they learnt.* By itself, knowledge does not equal success; it has to be put into action and this is definitely a business where the best way to learn and to succeed is to get on and do it.

   But there is no point in being teachable if the training you receive is inadequate. With most companies, training is in the hands of the distributors themselves and your sponsor and his or her uplines are critical in this. Therefore, the quality of support available to you can vary tremendously even within the same company. So, if you are going to be serious about your success in the business, I strongly suggest that you make sure that your sponsor is committed to the support you will need. Ask for the plan of action (what we call the *strategy*) for helping you to establish a successful business, *before* you commit yourself in writing to any company or sponsor. Most of it is set out in this book.

7. *They had patience.* Of course, any business, no matter what you do, requires time to build it and, in this respect, network marketing is no different. What is different is that, compared with many other businesses, the investment is comparatively low, the need to finance the growth of your business is non-existent (though you will need to invest in training materials to build up a network), and there are fewer external barriers to sales and income progression.

8. *They developed a sense of urgency.* This appears to conflict with a sense of patience but, in fact, it does not do so. There is no sense in being impatient because that is what causes corners to be cut and mistakes to be made. Impatience is a vice but 'urgency with patience' is a virtue.

9. *They became involved with the right company and the right product.* This is the subject of Chapter 5.

10. *They became users of the product.* As far as possible, distributors should buy and use the product for themselves. If their product is a consumable, they need to become their own best customers. Of course, this is a simplification and not always possible: a slim person may not need to take a course on slimming; a man who network markets cosmetics might prefer not to use the product on himself, and so on.

    This is a departure from traditional business where salespeople are rarely required to buy the products that their company supplies. However, a distributor is different in four respects:

- If you want people you know to buy your product, what sort of an example are you setting them if you do not use it yourself?
- You need to set an example to the rest of your group because, as your group gets bigger, an important part of your earnings will come from the purchases your distributors make for their own needs. If you do not use the product, why should they?
- A lot of retailing in network marketing is what is called 'passive' selling. That is, rather than you actively showing the product to people, people become interested in the product by happening to notice you using it. Even if they do not want the product for themselves, they may know someone who does.
- Passive selling does not lead merely to a sale of the product; it can lead to a chance for you to show the business opportunity to either your customer or to someone they know.

The fact is that if the product is not good enough for you to use, if you are not proud enough to want to use it, you should not be handling it.

11. *They set themselves clearly defined goals.* They had goals, not just for the business itself but, much more importantly, for the sort of lifestyle they wanted for themselves.

12. *They attend meetings regularly.* Meetings are key to success; they are the focal points around which the business revolves. The better the meetings, the more successful people's businesses become. Successful network marketeers place great emphasis not only on the quality of the meetings they run, but on encouraging their group to attend, support or run meetings. The importance of this is reflected by a saying in the business: 'No one ever succeeded by *not* going to meetings.'

13. *They were prepared to pay the price.* Whatever you want in life, there is a cost. Whatever success you want in business terms, the cost is in terms of the commitment you have to make. If you cannot make the commitment demanded by the reward, forget the reward. Only you can decide whether the reward is worth the effort. This may sound obvious, but many people who are used to being employed often find it difficult to accept that self-employment means that their level of success is down to them and no one else and, if they are used to receiving a regular wage or salary, self-employment means that they will not earn unless they produce. It is a harsh philosophy but a fair one; network marketing incomes

are geared directly to time input, effort and willingness to learn. There is no room for people who feel that the world owes them a living; this is a business for *net*workers, not *not*workers.

If you want to reach the top you must be prepared to make the same commitment you would have to make to get to the top in any field: total dedication of time and effort. Do not be led astray by promises made by some unscrupulous operators, 'Join now and, in one month, you could be collecting your Porsche!' In fact, you will have more chance of getting your Porsche if you steal it. There are huge returns to be made; many people have become independently wealthy in two to five years from starting, many others are on incomes of five figures per month; none got there without total dedication.

The consolation is that, once you have developed sufficient momentum in your network marketing business, you can ease off. It is going to roll on with or without you, bringing you a high return all the time. How long will this take? Anything from one to five years but, in any event, it is not a life sentence. This is in contrast to traditional business where, if you want to reach the top, you serve a life sentence of total dedication until you retire, or die first. If anything, it gets worse as you get older and as you get higher up the ladder.

Why do some people fail?

Network marketing is recognised as having a high drop-out rate and this can often put off, or at the least worry, interested people.

Not everyone is comfortable being self-employed

Of course, people do leave the business because, having tried it, they find that network marketing is the wrong career for them. Network marketing means self-employment and this, for those who have not been self-employed before, can be quite a culture shock. So be warned if you are about to embark on self-employment for the first time. Society brainwashes us into the belief that employment equates with security and self-employment with insecurity. Never mind that the actuality is the complete opposite because there is more security in depending on one's own actions than in being dependent on others; it is what people believe that matters.

There is comfort in knowing that there is a wage or salary at the end of the week and it is common to find people who cannot cope with the knowledge that what they earn at the end of the week is going to be entirely dependent on how successfully they are building their business.

Then, in many jobs people are surrounded all day by workmates; becoming a distributor will suddenly plunge them into a totally different environment involving long periods of 'aloneness'. Working from home, too, involves all sorts of disciplines and possibly family strains which working from an office, or being 'forced' to go out to work, does not. Executives and managers have to make the change from having others at their beck and call to being required to do everything themselves. Expecting other people to get results is much easier than having to achieve them oneself; people can become so used to 'telling, not doing' that, once they are thrown back on their own resources, they find that they are no longer capable of becoming producers themselves. *Be Your Own Boss!*, another title in this series, gives a good insight into self-employment and explains how to run a small business.

Although these are major reasons for dropping out, our concern here is not with people for whom network marketing was the wrong career or who find themselves uncomfortable with self-employment, but with what makes people fail despite genuinely wanting to succeed as distributors. If you know why people fail, that knowledge will help you to avoid the same pitfalls. Forewarned is forearmed.

The main reasons why people drop out

Given that someone wants to succeed and provided that they have taken care over their selection of a company and a product, all reasons for personal failure boil down to three basic causes:

- the distributor's attitude is wrong; or
- they do not fully understand the concept; or
- they do not apply it correctly.

The majority of drop-outs are unnecessary because they are the result of one of two avoidable causes.

First, a surprising number of people are simply not prepared to stick to the proven formula. Despite all the advice and warnings from those who have proved not only how to do it but also how *not* to do it, they choose to go their own way. A few are prepared to learn the hard way how important it is to stay on track, and it is remarkable how many of the top distributors have done this. But most will fail and blame their failure on the product, on the company, on network marketing, on their sponsor – in fact, on anything but themselves. Success comes from doing what successful people do and we covered the steps taken by successful people earlier in this chapter, but you will also find the positive steps to take in Chapter 8. Others drop out because they do not understand the importance of giving the geometric equation time to work; see page 25.

Second, and this is perhaps the single biggest cause of blame attaching to the industry, a large number of drop-outs are caused by amateurish upline support; if a person teaches someone else the wrong things, they are almost certainly guaranteeing that person's failure.

The recruitment system carries its own dangers

The biggest reason for the high drop-out rate inherent in network marketing is the result of the recruitment system. Think of the people whom you sponsor (leaving aside those who purely want to retail and who therefore do not want to build a business) as your sales directors, because each of them is building a separate sales business for you. If you were in traditional business and wanted to employ a sales director, you would place an advertisement in the newspaper. Let's say that you received 100 replies, would you offer every one of them the job of sales director? No, you would select one and reject 99.

But, in network marketing, you would offer all 100 the job. Any recruitment counsellor will tell you that, of the 100 applicants for any job, only ten will be capable of doing the job and that is true whether you are advertising for a petrol pump attendant or the chairman of a major corporation; in other words, you will get a 90 per cent failure rate anyway, whatever you do. And that is the average failure rate in network marketing – 90 per cent.

A more interesting statistic is that, of the people selected to do a job in traditional business, only 65 per cent succeed. So, after all the trouble of whittling down those 100 applicants to one, there is only a 65 per cent chance that you made a successful choice. Really, the best way of making sure that you had chosen the right sales director would be to take the whole lot on and then see who is left at the end . . . which is just what you do in network marketing!

There is an argument that the network marketing system is fairer on two counts: first, the selection process puts the power of choice into the hands of the applicant, not (as in traditional business) into the hands of the company; second, whereas in a normal business you would have room for only one sales director, network marketing allows every one of your 100 applicants to succeed if they have the determination to do so. So you can see that, because the system allows every applicant in, whereas traditional business allows only a few in, the drop-out rate is only apparently higher in network marketing.

Selecting a company and a product carefully is dealt with in Chapter 5.

5

What should you look for in the company and the product?

The company

It is so easy to be carried away by the excitement of a new proposition that even level-headed, experienced entrepreneurs – never mind those who are inexperienced in business – can, in the euphoria of the moment, overlook the most basic precautions.

If you decide to become a distributor, you are, even on a part-time basis, going to be putting a lot of effort and commitment into what is, after all, your own new business. So make sure that the company and the product you choose are going to deserve your efforts! It will pay you handsomely to remember two maxims from Jay Bertram:

- 'Your business cannot *long term* be more successful than the product.'
- 'An independent distributor cannot be more successful than his network marketing company.'

If you are looking at a new company, remember that no new company in any field will have a track record of success. So take time to look at the background of the directors. They do not need to have previous network marketing experience but what they must have is strong previous corporate experience. The growth in a new network marketing company can be truly phenomenal, far faster than is possible in normal business. One company I worked with sold £7 million worth of just one product in its first ten months and built a network of 9000 distributors. Cinergi was one of two companies launched in 1993 and which achieved 12,000 distributors in its first six months but was bankrupt a year later. The second company, Quorum, goes from strength to strength.

This explosive growth means that the directors have no time to learn how to steer a company as they go along. The time to learn to ski is not in the middle of an avalanche; if the board members do not already know how to practise their disciplines as directors (finance and accountancy, production and product development, sales and marketing, administration and computers, general management), they are likely to be swamped by the avalanche. But corporate experience is not enough; the team also need to be open-minded enough to accept that there are new lessons – or, perhaps more accurately, *attitudes* – to learn, without which they will not be successful. The point is that it is easier to graft the required knowledge of network marketing on to corporate experience than to try to do it the other way round.

You need to be sure that the company is operating according to the proper, ethical business principles of network marketing, not one of the corruptions of MLM. You need no longer fear the unethical aspects of pyramid selling because they are simply illegal. However, you do need to compare the company you are looking at with a matrix scheme or with a club membership or subscription selling scheme and we show you how to identify these in Chapter 6.

You should also avoid replying to any advertisements placed by distributors who are using an 0891 number. Not only does replying to these numbers cost you more than a normal telephone call, but the person who placed that advertisement makes a profit from British Telecom. If the distributor who placed the advertisement has a genuine need for anonymity, he or she can just as easily use a newspaper or Royal Mail box number, a secretarial agency or, best of all, an 0800 number.

Checklist

Go through the following checklist before you make your final decision.

- Are good administrative systems in place?
- Do they have a professional-looking brochure and sales aids?
- How quick is their delivery lead-time for orders?
- What is the out-of-stock position like?
- How complicated is the paperwork?
- How prompt are they at paying commission and how are you paid? (Methods and dates of payment vary from company to company.)
- What training do you get?
- How is it organised and what does it cost?

The Direct Selling Association codes

The Direct Selling Association, described in Chapter 8, expects its members to follow its Code of Business Conduct and its Code of Practice, which are reproduced below. These codes set standards for all companies in direct selling, whether they are members of the DSA or not.

Direct Selling Association Code of Business Conduct

This Code was adopted in 1991 to enable the direct selling of consumer goods in the UK to expand in an orderly manner. In 1991 the sales of Member Companies increased to £558 million and in doing so provided earnings opportunities for

490,000 men and women – predominantly on a part-time self-employed basis. The DSA recognises that, in view of the enormous range of consumer goods and services now being offered by direct selling businesses, the total business achieved by these companies will expand and at the same time offer many more opportunities to independent salespeople. The DSA believes that this Code will enable expansion to take place in a competitive but orderly environment.

1. Scope

This Code concerns a Member Company's dealings with:

(a) Its employed and self-employed people; and

(b) Other Member Companies.

2. Recruitment

2.1 Advertisements placed by either a Member Company or its independent salespersons shall not make extravagant earnings claims.

2.2 Advertisements shall not, for any reason, refer by name to any other direct selling company.

2.3 A Member Company shall neither promote nor endorse any direct or indirect recruitment activity offering employment or self-employment to persons known to be working with another Member company and shall actively dissuade its salespeople from making such approaches.

2.4 Any personal invitation, either verbal or written, to a presentation of a business opportunity shall:

(a) state the name of the company supplying the products and/or service and in any reference to the DSA shall state class of Membership

(b) not give the impression that it relates to an offer of employment or describe the event as anything other than an occasion to learn about a business opportunity.

2.5 All circulars, advertisements or other forms of communication whether written, audio, visual or otherwise, used for the purpose of recruitment or which teach methods of recruitment, must be approved in advance by the Member Company.

3. Presenting business opportunities

3.1 All face-to-face presentations of business opportunities in direct sales whether written, verbal or visual shall refer to the name of the company supplying the product or services and, in any reference to the DSA, state the class of Membership. (Only Members of the DSA are permitted to use the DSA logo and to state they are Members of the DSA.)

3.2 At all times during the presentation and events leading to a presentation of a business opportunity all Member Companies and their independent salespersons shall promote the opportunity as a business relationship with the Member Company and not with a person. Nor shall they suggest directly or indirectly, that the business opportunity, its products and/or services are part of any business other than the business of the Member Company.

3.3 During the presentation of a business opportunity no Member Company, or its salespersons, shall represent that benefits can be gained solely by introducing others and/or obtaining products for personal use or for demonstration purposes and must promote the business as an opportunity for every participant to retail products to end users at a realistic profit.

3.4 Personal testimonials of salespersons shall reflect actual earnings attributed to such individuals' activities, and shall not include commissions or earnings of other related salespersons.

3.5 Neither a Member Company nor their self-employed salespersons shall cause to denigrate nor to disseminate information about another direct selling company which may be harmful to that company.

4. Investments in business opportunities

4.1 Member Companies and independent salespersons working with Members shall not, at any time, permit an independent salesperson to purchase any more goods for resale than are needed to enable that independent salesperson to make demonstrations and personal sales on their own account and to meet customer orders that have been previously obtained.

4.2 Member Companies shall permit all independent salespersons to return goods for resale in merchantable condition for their net purchase price less a reasonable handling charge.

4.3 Members shall not permit any participant to qualify for a higher level of appointment in the distributorship structure unless a participant is able to provide proof that at least 50 per cent qualifying purchases are accounted for by sales of product to end users.

5. Code responsibilities

The chief executive of a Member Company shall be responsible for the observation of this Code by the Member Company, its employees and the independent salespersons working with it and for ensuring that a copy of this Code shall be supplied to all salespeople with the opportunity and/or responsibility for recruitment.

6. Code enforcement and administration

Breaches of this Code shall be dealt with in the first instance by the Director of the Association. If appropriate corrective action is not taken the matter shall be referred to a Select Committee of the Council. This Committee shall decide on the action to be taken by the Member Company concerned which, if not complied with, could lead to expulsion from Membership.

Direct Selling Association Code of Practice

MEMBERS' RESPONSIBILITIES

Methods of selling

1. Members shall satisfy the Association that effective measures are taken in the education of sales personnel with particular regard to their responsibilities to members of the public and their property. Members shall be adequately covered by a properly authorised insurance company to indemnify the public against any

claim as to personal injury or damage to property resulting from the demonstration or sale of goods.

2. Members who engage in party plan operations or who sell products to retail customers at business opportunity meetings shall provide invitation cards which make clear the purpose of the occasion and shall take all reasonable steps to ensure that party organisers and hostesses distribute them. Members shall also make clear in writing to party hostesses their rights and responsibilities.

3. Members shall take all reasonable steps to ensure their sales persons shall act with integrity and shall:

(a) present the sales features of their products to the customer both correctly and truthfully and shall respect the customer's right to privacy and to refuse further discussion.

(b) abide by the OFT's guidelines in the use of the telephone in both selling products and making appointments.

(c) ensure that technical and scientific information about products is truthfully and accurately presented and that advantage is not taken of customers' lack of knowledge.

(d) refrain from using the availability of personal incentives as a means of securing business.

(e) refrain from exploiting social, intellectual and emotional weaknesses in potential customers.

4. Members shall acquaint themselves with and observe all relevant legislation on trade and consumer protection.

Advertisements

5. Members' advertisements and promotional literature shall not contain any descriptions, claims or illustrations which directly or by implication are misleading about the product or service or about its suitability for the purpose recommended and shall comply strictly both with the British Code of Advertising Practice and the British Code of Sales Promotion Practice. Where Members use direct mail they will make use of the Mailing Preference Service.

Identification

6. All direct salespersons should immediately identify themselves to the prospective customer. They should indicate the purpose of their approach to the customer and identify the direct seller or manufacturer with whom they are associated and the product in which they deal.

7. The customer shall be given the name and address of the head office of the Member company and the name of the Member's local contact. Membership of the DSA shall be indicated. Copies of the Code of Practice shall be supplied to all agents and salespeople and shall be made available by them for perusal by customers.

Order forms

8. Members shall submit to the Association their order forms for inspection and approval. Such order forms shall:

   (a) contain the full name and address of the Member.

   (b) give details of the guarantee referred to in paragraph 9 below.

   (c) indicate that the company is a member of the Association (and, therefore, that it complies with this Code of Practice).

   (d) state the name and address of any local representative manager or responsible person to whom queries can be referred. A copy of the order shall be provided to the customer at the time when it is placed.

Guarantees

9. Members shall guarantee in writing the quality or fitness for purpose of their non-perishable merchandise to the customer. Such guarantees must not infringe the customer's rights under common or statute law. The guarantee should be clear, comprehensive and simple to understand. The terms of the guarantee shall be submitted to and approved by the Association bearing in mind the recommendations of the OFT on guarantees.

After-sales service

10. When an after-sales service is offered, details and limitations of such service must be clearly stated in writing. Where a customer would normally expect there to be after-sales service but where such service is not offered a statement in writing to this effect shall be given to the customer.

Rights of cancellation

11. Members shall ensure that customers are made aware of their rights of cancellation. Deposits and/or initial payments paid prior to delivery shall be refundable either in accordance with statutory requirements in the case of credit transactions, or on the cancellation of the order. Customers shall have a minimum of 14 days from the date of placing any order in which to cancel it.

CODE ADMINISTRATION

Code administration

12. This Code of Practice is under the supervision and administrative control of an independent legally qualified Code Administrator who will report annually on the administration of the Code.

13. The Code Administrator shall satisfy himself that Members' documentation and trading practices comply with the Code and relevant legislation. Where a breach of the Code or the law is identified he shall advise the Member and if the matter is not rectified within a reasonable period he shall report it to the Council of the Association.

14. No fees or charges are payable by any complainant. It is expected that any query or complaint about goods or services supplied by a Member Company of the Association shall be made in the first place to that company.

15. Each year the Chief Executive of every Member company will be required to sign a Code of Practice Compliance Certificate and undertake to comply with any judgement of the Code Administrator in any matter relating to the sale of goods other than product liability claims.

Complaint procedure

16. In the case of a product complaint where the customer fails to obtain satisfaction and complains to the Association, the following procedure is adopted:

    (a) The complainant is requested to complete a form setting out the relevant details.

    (b) On receipt by the Association of the completed form, a copy is sent to the senior executive of the Company requesting prompt remedial action. At the same time the customer is advised of the action being taken.

    (c) If the Association has not been informed in writing that the matter has been resolved within 21 days of the letter being sent to the Member Company then:

    (i) details of the complaint, including the completed form, are referred to the Code Administrator.

    (ii) details of the complaint are reported to the Council of the Association.

    (iii) if the complaint has not been resolved by the Code Administrator within 28 days of the complaint being referred to him, the complaint is again referred to the Council of the Association together with reasons for the delay in reaching agreement.

    (iv) following the initial 28-day period allowed to the Code Administrator to reach an agreement, the Council of the Association will allow a further 28 days for the Code Administrator to adjudicate between the complainant and the Member Company and to settle the matter.

    With regard to any other breach of the Code which cannot be resolved by the Association then the matter shall be referred to the Code Administrator who shall investigate and report thereon to the Council.

Sanctions

17. The Code Administrator shall have the power to impose any or all of the following sanctions in cases where a Member has been held to contravene the Code and/or to be in breach of contract.

    (a) To require complete restitution to the customer of monies paid for the products.

    (b) To require the replacement or repair of the product.

    (c) To require the payment of any costs incurred by the Code Administrator for technical advice or testing.

    (d) To require the Member to submit to the Code Administrator a written undertaking to abide by the Code of Practice and to exercise all due diligence in preventing a recurrence of the breach.

    (e) To award fair and reasonable damages.

On the recommendations of the Code Administrator disciplinary action will be taken by the DSA which may ultimately lead to expulsion from the DSA.

Redress

18. Members and customers may at any stage seek help and guidance from Trading Standards Officers, Consumer Advice Centres or Citizens' Advice Bureaux and pursue their normal legal rights and seek redress from the County Courts in England, Wales and Northern Ireland or the Sheriff Courts in Scotland.

Codes reproduced by kind permission of the Direct Selling Association.

The product

Many distributors, if they are not from a commercial background, can misunderstand the importance of the product to the success of their business. Some networks place so much emphasis on business-building by sponsoring that the issue of how good the product is can become clouded.

Traditional companies use trained salespeople, sometimes heavy advertising and sales promotion to sell their products. This means that the quality of the product is not as important as the amount of money poured into making it sell. As a result, you will find plenty of examples where the fastest-selling product is not the best in that particular price-band; it is the one which has had the most money put behind it. For instance, where do you get the tastiest eggs, bacon and sausages from: your local supermarket or a good local dealer? Yet who has the higher sales?

But network marketing uses an entirely different philosophy of retailing: people 'recommend' a product to friends, relations, neighbours and acquaintances, or to people introduced to them by friends, relations, neighbours or acquaintances. If you are going to recommend a product to someone you know, or someone who has been introduced to you by a friend, how will you need to feel about the product? Will you not need to feel that it is at least as good as anything else at that price on the market? It is for this reason that good companies place such reliance on the quality of the product. In network marketing, 95 per cent of distributors neither are, nor want to be, trained salespeople. If they do not feel good about the product they will soon stop recommending it.

So have a good look at the product. First, is it the sort of product which excites you? Is it the sort of product you would feel good about showing to people you know? If not, move on! Enthusiasm about what you are dealing in is vital to your enjoyment and essential to your success. No one of integrity ever succeeded by promoting products they did not feel good about to people they know!

If you like the look of the product, find out what product guarantees the company gives. Obviously, products need to comply with the Trade Descriptions Act (in other words, be of merchantable quality, last a reasonable time, and so on) and with any other relevant legal requirements but, realistically, this is difficult to check out without being pedantic.

But it is not enough to feel comfortable with recommending the product, the people you recommend it to must also want to buy it. There are some excellent products on the market with only one fault: no one wants to buy them. There are many instances where the general public are not attracted to a particular product and the only people buying it are existing distributors or people just joining the network. If this happens, the product will eventually clog up the network and this means, in the end, that you are not going to earn much money from it.

If the market for that product is already well established, all you need to do is see how its price and presentation compare with other, similar, products in the shops. Be careful that you are comparing like with like; you cannot compare the price of a Rolls-Royce with that of a Lada, yet both cars have a good market. If the so-called *quality/price ratio* (that is, how a product's price compares with other products of similar quality) is good, you should find it easy to sell. Try to find out whether the company has product development plans to keep abreast at least, if not ahead, of the market; and whether there are new lines coming on stream. For reasons of commercial security, the company may refuse to divulge much information but you should be able to get a feel as to whether it is forward thinking in product terms, or resting on its laurels.

If the product is unique, it is more difficult to find out if there is a market for it. Asking people you know is not a good way to establish this because, at this stage, you know very little about the product – you may not even have a sample – and you certainly do not know enough to show it to other people; the result is that they may turn down an idea on the basis of your description whereas, had you shown it to them properly, they might have thought it an excellent idea and worth buying. I could put anyone off buying a Rolls-Royce; it would be much more difficult if they were sitting in it. Conversely, some people think that an idea is a great one until you turn up with the product to sell to them; then you find that they meant that it was a great idea for everyone else to buy, but not for them.

It is a fallacy that 'unique' products necessarily network better. The new and unique product which the company is raving about may be a great idea, but do people want to buy it? The real criterion is whether it has a ready market, not whether it is unique.

It is also a fallacy that repeat products are necessarily better than so-called 'one-off' sales. Network marketing is simply another way to retail the product. Just as there are traditional retailers earning a good living from selling one-off products such as televisions, kitchen utensils and cars, so there are plenty of high-earning independent distributors handling one-off products. One-off products are also called consumer durables. They do repeat-sell, but over a longer time-frame.

Much more important than whether it is a repeat product or a one-off is the question: are you going to feel proud of it? If not, look for an alternative. Some people feel comfortable with one product, some with another. There is no right or wrong here, only whether you feel comfortable with it.

To sum up:

- Whether the product is mass consumable (that is, with a high repeat value) or consumer durable (a one-off sale), distributors must be users of the product themselves, as far as possible. If it is a mass consumer product, they must be happy to keep using or 'consuming' it themselves, so that everyone keeps earning from repeat orders.
- In any event, the product must retail easily outside the network, which means it must have a ready market to people who are not distributors.

Dealing with problems

What can you do if, after all this, by mischance you get involved with a poor company?

Or what happens if, more likely, your upline (the person who sponsored you) is not as ethical as his company is? Bear in mind that successful companies will have a large number of distributors and, while a good company will act fast once it finds a distributor breaks the contract or the ethical codes, it is impossible for it to police so many people.

There is a 14-day cooling-off period which starts from when you sign the agreement (see page 72. If you find the problem within this time, you are entitled to all your money back and you should contact the company direct.

If the problem is more sinister, for instance, your sponsor has run off with your money, normal civil and criminal laws apply. Your lawyer might advise you to take your sponsor to the civil courts, but this is often more trouble than it is worth. I would suggest you take the following steps:

1. Advise the company what has happened. Although you may have no legal claim against them, they may well prefer to reimburse you rather than have adverse publicity.
2. If this does not work, report your sponsor to the police because he is

guilty of a criminal act. You may still not get any money back but you will stop other people from being exploited.

If the problem is not with your sponsor but with the company

1. Advise the DSA whose address is on page 67. Even if the company are not DSA members, they can advise you.
2. Report the company to your local DTI office and possibly the local Office of Fair Trading. Yellow Pages will give you the local office.

What happens in the event of company bankruptcy?

If you are not used to the business world, this may be worrying you. The strongest companies can get into difficulties very fast; the company you join could (unknown to you) be in serious cash difficulties now but, within months, with good management, could be in a very strong position. If you are going to worry about this, the only answer, frankly, is to join no company inside or outside network marketing, because even world experts could not guarantee that any particular company will be here next year – or that this, very weak company, will not be thriving next year! Bankruptcies are facts of business life.

However, if this unfortunate event occurs, you will have a claim against the company, along with all the other creditors, but the chances are that, realistically, there will not be much money in the kitty to share around. Write in and stake your claim. What you should *not* do is incur legal fees in pursuing your claim but do make sure that you fill in all the requisite forms which will be sent to you by the insolvency expert dealing with the affairs of the company.

What happens if one of your customers wants to return goods?

If the complaint is genuine – in other words, the goods are faulty, out of date code, not as advertised or not suitable for the purpose for which they were intended – the normal legal situation of supplying non-merchantable goods applies. The customer can either ask for a replacement or a refund. This must be honoured by you, as the immediate supplier, but the company must also reimburse you.

Customers who order direct, whether by mail order or by a salesperson, agent or distributor, legally have 14 days in which they can simply change their mind and have a refund from you, provided the goods have not been used. If the goods have been used, the customer must prove that they were not of merchantable quality. If they simply change their mind, you have no recourse against your company but my experience of dealing with many such situations is that, first, it is extremely rare for a customer to want a refund *for no reason* and, second, if it does happen, it was usually the fault of the distributor, the classic case being that the distributor did not show a sample, so what the customer got was not what they expected.

6
What systems should you avoid?

'It is no more sensible to judge this business by its abusers than it is to judge the medical profession or the building business by their rogues.' (Jay Bertram)

That said, there is no doubt that, because the entry requirement for companies is low compared to high-level normal business and because it is so much easier to set up a company, MLM attracts more than its fair share of scoundrels. Provided that you take the trouble to learn a little about the concept, this should not cause you any difficulty and it is certainly not a reason *not* to get involved. Once you have read this chapter, you will find that the corruptions of MLM are, in fact, easy to spot and steer clear of.

Pyramid selling

The law is confusing because it defines all forms of MLM as pyramid selling, and then makes illegal certain unethical aspects of it. The MLM industry and this book uses the term 'pyramid selling' to refer to certain unacceptable aspects of MLM.

Pyramid selling did, in fact, use the traditional form of distribution, product physically moving down a chain of distributors until it reached the consumer. However, there was one apparently small but crucial difference: unlike traditional retailing, there was no set retail price and therefore no means of stopping the product going way over its proper retail value as it moved down the chain. The result was catastrophic and created such a harmful business concept that, although it was outlawed as long ago as 1973 (by the Fair Trading Act, Part IX, as amended by the Pyramid Selling Schemes Regulations 1989 and the Pyramid Selling Schemes [Amendment] Regulations 1990; currently, the DTI is seeking yet more changes to the law), the legacy of the damage which pyramid selling caused tainted the industry for the next 20 years. Although the recession has been tragic for so many people, one 'good' result, if I may use the term, is that many serious business and professional people, who in the past would have treated network marketing with disdain, have been forced to look at it as the only realistic escape for themselves from the morass of bankruptcy, financial hardship or redundancy, and network marketing is being taken extremely seriously by many aware people and organisations.

So how did pyramid selling cause the problem it did? Figure 6.1 will show

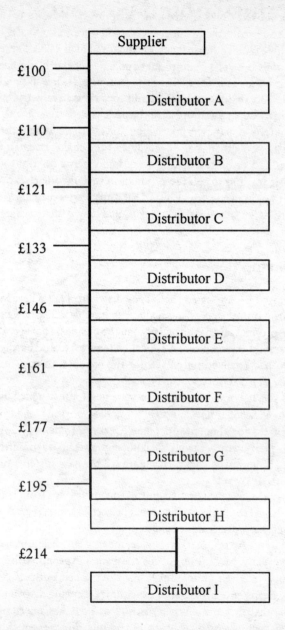

Figure 6.1 *How stock and price moved in pyramid selling*

you how the product moved down a chain of distributors. Because each distributor had to make a profit, the product increased in price as it went.

As you can see, in this example the product left the supplier at £100. There are tremendous variations between one product and another but it is a fair assumption that, if a product sells for £100 at the factory gate, it will retail in the shops at around £200. In our example, distributor H was already trying to sell the product to distributor I at more than the price that product would sell at in the shops. Therefore, with pyramid selling, it was not a case that the system might fail, it was worse than that – every line of the chain was *bound* to fail because a point had to be reached in every line when a distributor found it was impossible for him to sell the product on to someone else. So the real problem was that, in every case, it was a certainty that a distributor would be caught with large amounts of stock – and could do nothing about it.

How did the law stop this?

It stopped it very simply. The law stated that, if any distributor anywhere in the chain wanted to drop out, the company had to pay him back 90 per cent of what he paid for the product, even if he had been in the business for several years. Now, even if pyramid selling were an ethical system, you could hardly expect a supplier, who had received only £100 for the product, to pay out £192.60 (90 per cent of £214) to distributor I for it!

The answer which the network marketing companies found (which is what all the ethical ones were doing anyway) was, first, to set standard wholesale and retail prices for their products and, second, to arrange for most of the distributors to buy direct from the company instead of from the next distributor above them in the chain. In Figure 6.2 the two systems of distribution are shown side by side

As in traditional business, the more a distributor's business buys from the company, the bigger the extra wholesale discounts he receives. For the sake of clarity, the diagram takes no account of these.

You can see that, on the network marketing side, most of the distributors buy direct from the company. Most (but not all) companies expect distributors to draw their stock from an upline until they reach a certain level of promotion, and I have represented this in our example by showing distributor I being supplied by distributor H. When distributor I reaches a certain sales turnover, he, too, will bypass distributor H and buy direct from the company. It is very much in distributor H's interests to build up distributor I's business to the point where this happens because he will continue to earn

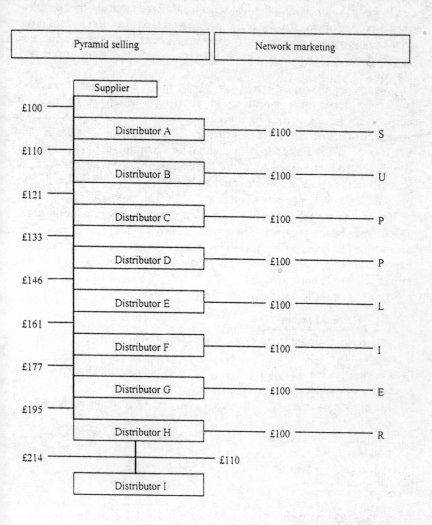

Figure 6.2 *Comparison between pyramid selling and network marketing*

royalty or commission on distributor I's sales, and may even get some whole-sale discount despite no longer supplying distributor I.

However, some pyramid selling schemes suffered from another problem: they were set up so that the main income was from enrolment fees rather than the movement of product. The law largely banned that as well, and now generally the only means of earning is from the proper sale and purchase of stock.

Pyramid selling thus negated two of the major advantages of network marketing. First, there is nothing but short-term benefit to be gained in network marketing by buying more stock than what is necessary to meet your immediate needs; this means that someone with no money has as good a chance of succeeding as someone who is wealthy; but, in pyramid selling, the more product you bought, the higher the position you obtained for yourself in the chain, so people could make money only if they already had, or could borrow, large sums of money.

Second, in network marketing, you promote yourself automatically as the size of your business grows: you do not have to buy more stock to achieve promotion because you are pushed up by the expansion of your group; but, in pyramid selling, the only way to promote yourself was to invest yet more money in buying more stock.

So, to sum up, the two systems compare as follows:

Pyramid selling	Network marketing
1. A large investment to make big money	Minimum investment
2. Distributors were caught with huge stock	Legal buy-back insurance
3. Major income from enrolments	No income from enrolments
4. Self-promotion virtually non-existent	Self-promotion a major plus point
5. Prices set by your position in the chain	Set buying and selling prices

Matrixes or matrices

Matrices are a second form of MLM to avoid. They have two hallmarks:

- Unlike network marketing, where a distributor can have as many or as few frontliners (people he has sponsored) as he likes; the structure of a matrix is fixed by the company. For example, a 5 × 7 matrix means that your matrix goes five distributors wide and seven distributors deep in each line. This means that you and your people can have neither more nor less than five frontliners each.

- As a result, it is impossible to have a 'self-promotion' system, thus negating one of the biggest attractions of network marketing to anyone with any ambition (see page 33). So, unlike a network marketing group, which is remarkably fluid and flexible, the matrix has a rigid and inflexible structure:

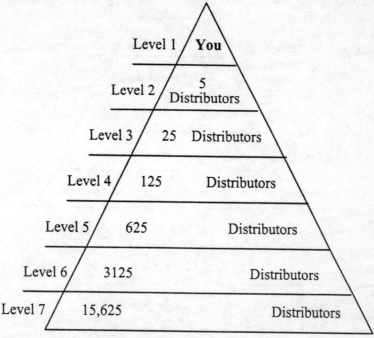

Figure 6.3 *A 5 by 7 matrix*

You can see that it looks as if your matrix grows with satisfying speed. And, indeed, in theory it does because you have achieved a total of 15,625 distributors in your matrix, even though each person has only sponsored five others.

But in practice it is not as easy as that. You will find that you need to sponsor many more than your five people in order to fill the large gaps left by the majority of distributors, who will find only one or two – or perhaps nobody.

Some schemes put you back in lower down in your own matrix with no additional registration fee required. This sounds like a generous gesture to reward your efforts by giving you extra opportunities to earn. The reality is that you will already have contacted everyone you can possibly think of just to get down that far, so putting you back into your own matrix means that, unless you can conjure up a lot of names from somewhere, you are going to be left with a 'hole' in your matrix:

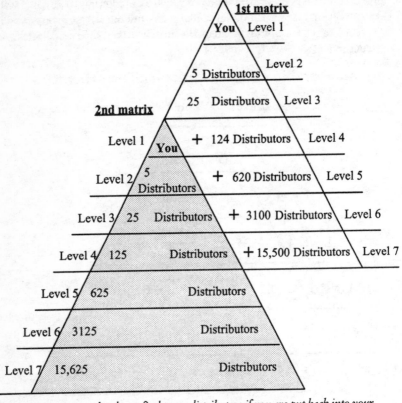

Figure 6.4 *It is even harder to find more distributors if you are put back into your matrix lower down*

You can see that the 'generosity' of putting you back into your own matrix in fact almost guarantees that you will not be able to fill it.

In some schemes, the company may pay out nothing on, for example, your first three levels. Because it knows that few distributors last long enough to earn, it has created a sales force at almost no expense to itself.

In others, you can only make the big money by filling in your bottom level. Since few distributors survive long enough to complete anywhere near their bottom levels, the company has virtually guaranteed saving itself this pay-out.

Therefore, matrices work heavily in the company's favour. In fact, whereas all *properly run* network marketing companies can show you high earners, I have never heard of a high earner in a matrix; and none of the *long-lasting* high-level companies uses a matrix.

After close on 50 years of trying, both the USA and the UK are still awaiting the first long-lasting company which got there by using a matrix. Given this lack of success and that countless thousands of people have lost money and valuable time getting involved in matrix schemes, there is a strong argument in favour of banning them.

Club membership or subscription-selling schemes

In such schemes you are paid on the sale of club memberships. The product is usually something like membership of a wine or spirits club, or a club offering discounts across a wide variety of goods, or for specific products like records, CDs or videos. As there is no real difference between paying distributors for recruiting people (which is largely illegal) and paying them for recruiting someone into a 'club', because either way you are paid on people rather than product, it is questionable how legal these schemes are.

Whether legal or not, no such schemes (whether using MLM or direct selling techniques) have yet stood the test of time for an obvious reason: distributors earn nothing from the movement of stock and therefore make no effort to sell the products. Despite this, you might think that customers would take advantage of the discounts or other club benefits, especially as it cost good money to join the club and even more especially because some of the discounts offered are substantial. But in reality this is not the case; direct sales of any sort depend much more on the personal contact than the prices people pay. In the absence of a distributor promoting the product, the customer soon reverts to the local shop.

Most club membership schemes also use a matrix system. We have already seen that no high-level matrix system has stood the test of time in either the USA or the UK, so any company using both systems is therefore putting two obstacles in the way of its success.

Chain letter systems

These schemes either have no product at all, or they use an inferior product as an excuse for passing money up the chain. Favourite schemes are to offer either badly written books on 'how to succeed' (or some other equally compelling sounding title) or subscriptions to magazines on business opportunities.

These systems, unlike network marketing and in common with matrices, have no self-promotion element and do not offer the opportunity to build a proper, long-lasting business.

7

What does it cost to get started?

At whatever level you want to become involved, this is not a business which requires much capital. You need a telephone and a fixed address to start with.

All reputable distributors (under the guidance of their network marketing company) will make it clear to you that the only stock you ought to buy is that legitimately needed for samples or demonstration, but they are not legally allowed to make you buy even that. All other stock need be bought only after you have received an order for it. In this way, people with no money are not at a disadvantage.

To protect you further, the company is not legally allowed to accept more than £75 (including VAT) as a total of all payments (enrolment fee, stock, samples, sales aids and anything else they can think of) in your first seven days. After that, there are no restrictions on what you can buy. The company also cannot legally require you to attend any training for which you have to pay a fee, although it is clearly in your own interests to accept as much training as you can.

As a further safeguard, if you drop out at any time, even after several years in the business, you can legally require your company to buy back the stock from you at 90 per cent of what you paid for it, provided, of course, that it is unopened, undamaged and unused. There can be few business where the supplier can be forced to buy back stock for no reason.

In many network marketing opportunities, you can (as in normal business) qualify for a higher discount by buying a quantity of stock; but it is not worth doing this unless you have spare money available. Although you are taking little risk (because of the 90 per cent buy-back clause), there is no sense in depriving yourself in order to do this and it is always advisable to keep expenses down until you see how it is going to go.

Buying a lot of stock may also promote you up the ladder. There may seem to be an advantage in doing this, but in fact any benefits are no more than short term. After a few months, you cannot normally tell whether someone bought in at a higher level or came in with the minimum stock possible. However, despite the lack of long-term advantage, some people feel happier with the status of coming in at a higher level, and there is nothing wrong with that.

So you should resist all pressures to buy more than you feel comfortable with. In fact, if any pressure is put on you to buy more, your sponsor is not behaving in accordance with the ethics of the concept and, if the company is an ethical one, he is acting outside its instructions too.

Although the entry requirement (how much money you need to get started) is low, that may not be all the money you will need. If your intention is to retail rather than business-build, this should not be a major problem: selling network marketed products is no different from selling any other products except that, generally, each sale will earn you more.

But, if your intention is to business-build, your new business is going to cost you perhaps a lot more than the registration fee and any samples or stock that you decide to buy. These are the *hidden costs* and they cover such things as telephone calls, postage, travelling costs, possibly printing or administration, aids to help you with your sponsoring such as books or videos (which you lend to people you know). If your aim is to build a serious business, there is no point in coming into a new career without bothering to learn about it, so don't forget the trainings, books, videos and tapes which you should invest in; these should not add up to much but they need to be allowed for. And, of course, don't forget that you need money to live on.

If you are mainly sponsoring, rather than retailing, it can in some instances take a while to generate a living income, so you need to feel that you can keep going financially until your income is sufficient to cover your outgoings (living and business expenses). We need to differentiate here between how much money you *would like* to earn and how much money you *must have* to survive – the latter is your first concern. Some people need to earn straight away, others can keep going for a long while either on private capital or because they have an income from another occupation, or because their spouse is earning enough to keep the two of them while the network marketing business builds up.

Therefore, even though a good immediate income from sponsored sales is difficult, you should feel comfortable that you can either earn sufficient from building a business quickly through that route, or make the income you need from retailing, or ensure that you have enough capital to keep you going until you reach break-even point (when your income equals your outgoings or expenses).

If your present financial circumstances are such that you have to earn a significant figure from your network marketing business very soon, you should discuss carefully with your sponsor *before* you sign up how best to achieve this. There is no point in signing up, only to find that your immediate income needs are such that you cannot meet them in this business. Bear in mind that no sponsor in any company can guarantee how much money you will make; all the company does is to provide you with the framework but, within that, it is impossible to forecast what you will earn and when – in the same circumstances, some distributors earn a lot within weeks, others will not achieve the same in years; it really is down to you at the end of the day.

But what your sponsor should be able to do is to demonstrate that there is a *realistic* potential for you to earn what you need and what steps you must take to unleash that potential. If he cannot do that, look elsewhere.

The safest course is to have an assured income from another source and build your business part time until you feel confident that you can convert it to a full-time business. However, this is not always possible and going straight into network marketing full time, although not the perfect solution, is often a case of 'needs must'. If you are in that position, take comfort from the fact that many people before you have had to do the same thing and have made themselves independently wealthy within a few years.

8
So, what do you do next?

Network marketing is not necessarily right for everyone; there is no such thing as an occupation, job, career or business which is. It is not important whether, in the end, you get involved or not. What is important is that you make the right decision for yourself. This book can only give you the foundations for arriving at the right decision. If you want to investigate the possibilities more deeply and this book was lent to you by a distributor, he or she will arrange this for you. If that is not an option, there are a variety of other ways in which you can track down likely companies:

There are two trade organisations, both of which have network marketing members:*

- The Direct Selling Association (DSA), 29 Floral Street, London WC2E 9DP; 071–497 1234
- The Network Marketing Association (NMA), 5 Cornwall Crescent, London W11 1PH; 071–221 5611

There are excellent companies which belong to neither organisation and you can find details of these in several magazines which specialise in business opportunities or what are called 'home businesses' (of which network marketing is one). The two current leaders are:

- *Home Business*, 14 Hove Business Centre, Fonthill Road, Hove BN3 6HA; 0273 888992
- *The New Entrepreneur* (TNE), Sylvan House, Glenmoriston, Inverness IV3 6YJ; 0320 40210

Apart from the advertisements for network marketing companies which these magazines carry, you may also find profiles of companies you are looking into in back numbers – as, indeed, you may in *BusinessAge* which is a high-level magazine for business people and also promotes network marketing. Their address is 96–98 Baker Street, London W1M 1LA; 071–487 5057. In addition to these, you will find advertisements for network marketing companies in most newspapers and periodicals which have business opportunity sections in their classified advertisements.

---

* Please note that UK telephone area codes are due to change on 16 April 1995. Check the numbers in this book that you wish to use after that date.

Steps to take before you decide to sign up

1. *Ask if the company you are looking at runs meetings* specially designed for people looking at the business for the first time. These meetings are called different things by different companies but some typical names are 'business opportunity meetings' (BOMs for short), 'showcases', 'briefings' and so on. If they are held, you might find that going to one and seeing, not only what it is all about, but also the sort of people who get involved, would help you before you make a final decision. It's easy to get carried away on a tide of euphoria, so take time to cool off.

2. Unless your circumstances are very similar to those of your sponsor, *ask if you can meet another distributor with whom you may have common ground*, perhaps a distributor from the same social, educational or ethnic background, or with a similar work history to yourself. If you feel that you may have particular problems to overcome in order to succeed as a distributor, it can help if you get your sponsor to introduce you to someone else who has had to overcome similar problems. I suppose that the major doubt most people have is not whether the concept works or not, but whether they can make it work for them, so talking to people whose experience will match yours is a great confidence booster.

   If you find that you happen to get on better with one of the other distributors than with the person who is introducing you to the business, I should mention that it is not considered acceptable to change sponsors! Network marketing only works if distributors have total trust in each other and just about the biggest crime which can be committed is for one distributor to steal another's contact. No properly run company would allow this, and no ethical distributor would agree to it. If either do, you will almost certainly find that you have made the wrong choice.

3. *See how you feel about the product and check it out properly.* I laid out the guidelines for this in Chapter 5.

4. Discuss with your sponsor *how much support you will receive to get your business going*. Both your sponsor and several people upline of him or her will earn a royalty or commission on your sales, so this is not a favour you are asking for: it is your entitlement. If people are going to earn from your efforts, make sure that they work for it and give you all the support you want. In my experience, the great majority of uplines are only too anxious to help. Their problem is that not enough people want it, preferring to take all the risks and make all the same mistakes inherent in trying to go it alone.

Don't worry if your sponsor is relatively inexperienced because, if you are joining a good group, sponsor and uplines all work as a team to help you to get your business off the ground. However, if your sponsor is inexperienced, it becomes even more important to make sure before you start that there are experienced uplines (or, if you are looking at a start-up company, experienced members of the corporate team) available to help you.

5. *Do not be worried by the marketing plan.* It has nothing to do with how you market the products; it is how you earn your money and is trade jargon for the 'payment and promotion plan'. It is usually difficult to grasp the concept when you are outside the organisation, but you do need to be sure that you are not becoming involved with a matrix scheme (see Chapter 6). When you start introducing your own distributors to the network, you will need to be able to explain the outline to them, but by then you will have become more knowledgeable.

Even experienced distributors waste far too much time on trying to judge a business by its marketing plan, but the fact that one company pays more or less percentage than another is not relevant. The percentage you earn is not important, it is the saleability of the product which is the important thing and you will be better off earning a lower percentage on a product which sells well than a higher percentage on a product which turns out to be difficult to sell. If it is a start-up company the most experienced network marketeer in the world will not be able to tell if the plan is good or not in practice – only time will tell and, if it is not, the company will soon change it.

6. If the company or the group you are joining runs training sessions for new distributors you can, if you so wish, *attend one of these before signing up.* There is nothing either particularly for or against attending a training session before (rather than after) you sign up. It is more a case of whether you will feel more comfortable if you do. It is normal and acceptable for fees to be charged for trainings.

7. *Be careful how you discuss it with your friends.* If you sign up, you may well want to approach your friends either with the opportunity or as customers for the product, and the time to do that is when you know all about it. To approach them before may be counter-productive.

The contract

All network marketing companies are required by law to give you a contract, some of which has to be formatted in a legally required way. They are also required by law to include certain clauses. A specimen is shown on pages 72-76. However, non-statutory clauses may vary. You should look to see whether either the contract or your sponsor bring the following points to your attention:

1. That you have the right to require the company to buy back your stock at any time for 90 per cent of what you paid for it, provided, of course, that is undamaged, in its original packaging and suitable for resale as new. *For this reason, you should never take stock out of its original packaging* unless you specifically need it as a sample or are actually going to use it. In the case of buy-backs, all uplines have to pay back the wholesale discounts and royalties they originally received on that stock, so one of the tricks of unethical sponsors is to get new distributors to open up all their stock, thus ensuring that it cannot be sold back.

2. That you are not required to buy any stock until you have sold it.

3. That if you are intending to promote yourself immediately to a higher position on the marketing plan by buying the extra stock required, there will be no long-term advantage to you.

4. That you do not have to attend trainings for which a fee is required.

5. That you should not be asked to pay more than £75 as a total of all payments in your first seven days.

6. That you have a 14-day 'cooling-off period' during which you may cancel the contract and have refunded all the money you have paid out. But do note that, if you do this, most companies will not allow you to reregister for at least a year.

7. That a high income is not guaranteed.

8. That any claims of income actually earned can be substantiated.

9. The distributor can terminate the agreement by giving the requisite notice to the company, with a copy to the sponsor, as set out in his contract. If this happens within 14 days of start-up, the distributor can ask for all payments made to be refunded provided materials supplied are returned in a resaleable condition. In the event of cancellation for whatever reason, the distributor may be barred from taking up a new distributorship with that company for a year.

10. The law requires the contract to state that you should seek professional advice before entering into any agreement. Be sure that your legal adviser is familiar with network marketing, and knows what he is talking about. A divorce lawyer, for example, may be zealous in protecting the client's interests but not know much about commercial business. A better option is to have the adviser included in the discussions. I find that advisers are noticeably more careful about the advice they give if they are included in the sponsoring process.

11. The next stage, if you are happy with the company, the product and the support your sponsor is going to give to you, is to sign up and pay your registration fee. (This is an annual fee and may go up from time to time.)

Steps to take after you have signed up

1. *Decide with your sponsor how much stock you want to start with.* As we saw earlier, you cannot legally be required to buy any stock or samples. This means that you only have to buy stock after you have already pre-sold it. Remember that you are not allowed to pay the company more than £75 including VAT in your first seven days, and this includes any payments you have made for registration, administration or sales aids, as well as stock. This rule, while it is designed to stop new people being taken advantage of by unscrupulous companies or distributors, is extremely irksome to someone who wants to get his or her business going as fast as possible. It is even more irksome to someone who has financial problems and therefore wants to start selling as soon as possible. That is why you should avoid further delays by ordering the stock you want as soon as you sign up.

   While companies cannot make anyone buy stock unless they have already sold it, it is a poor salesperson who sells without samples and therefore you should invest in as good a range of samples as you can afford without getting yourself into financial difficulties. In some companies which depend upon sales by using catalogues, it is claimed that you do not need to buy samples at all because it is all in the catalogue. Any experienced salesperson will tell you that those distributors who do buy samples of what is in the catalogue will sell more than those who do not.

   It is an important part of the concept of network marketing that distributors should themselves be users of the product. Simply using the product yourself will get you sales from people who see you doing this. (Continued on page 76.)

INDEPENDENT DISTRIBUTOR APPLICATION FORM

(OFFICE USE ONLY) ID Number ☐☐☐☐

The ID Number of the Sponsor...... ☐☐☐

The Surname of theSponsor:
☐☐☐☐☐☐☐☐

The Initials of the Sponsor...... ☐☐

The Date of this Application is...... ☐☐/☐☐/9☐

STATUTORY WARNING

Before you sign the contract:

(a) Make sure that you have read it carefully and that you have seen a document which explains the scheme in detail.

(b) Consider the following:

1. It is advisable to take independent legal advice before signing a contract.

2. Do not be misled by claims that high earnings are easily achieved.

3. All businesses carry some risk. Do not purchase more stock than you believe you can sell in a reasonable period.

IF THE SPONSOR IS NOT A MARKETING ID, the Name of the next one is ☐☐☐☐☐☐☐☐☐

This Application, if accepted by _____ Limited, will constitute the Agreement between _____ Limited of the above address (hereinafter called The Promoter) and the Independent Distributor (hereinafter called The Distributor) whose details are as below.

SURNAME OF DISTRIBUTOR ☐☐☐☐☐☐☐☐☐☐☐ DOB ☐☐/☐☐/19☐☐

FORENAMES ☐☐☐☐☐☐☐☐☐ TITLE ☐☐☐☐☐

BONUSES AND INVOICES TO BE MADE OUT TO ☐ ☐☐☐☐☐☐☐☐

SPOUSE'S SURNAME ☐☐☐☐☐☐☐☐☐☐ FORENAMES ☐☐☐☐☐☐☐☐☐☐

IS YOUR SPOUSE A PARTNER IN THIS BUSINESS? ☐YES ☐NO TEL.☐☐☐☐☐☐☐☐

ADDRESS ☐☐☐☐☐☐☐☐☐☐☐☐☐☐☐☐☐☐☐☐

TOWN ☐☐☐☐☐☐☐☐☐ COUNTY ☐☐☐☐☐☐☐

POSTCODE ☐☐☐☐☐☐ PHONE ☐☐☐☐☐☐☐☐☐

I hereby acknowledge that I have read and understood the front and the back of this contract. I understand that I may not order products (including the registration fee, the Business Pack and any administration) at a cost to me exceeding £75.00 (including VAT) within 7 days of the date of this agreement and the Promoter confirms that no monies received from the Distributor shall be construed as a non-returnable deposit for goods.

SIGNATURE OF THE DISTRIBUTOR _____

(If signing on behalf of a limited company, please state position)

SIGNATURE OF THE SPOUSE (If in partnership with Distributor). I hereby confirm

that I am equally bound by the terms of this Application as if I was the Distributor _____

SIGNATURE OF SPONSOR _____

SIGNED ON BEHALF OF THE PROMOTER _____

ACCESS/VISA/MASTERCARD

Card No.: ☐☐☐☐☐☐☐☐☐☐☐☐☐☐☐☐

Expiry date: ☐☐/☐☐

Name as on card:

Top Copy to Office with Registration fee. Blue copy to Distributor. Yellow copy to Sponsor

RULES OF OPERATION OF AN INDEPENDENT DISTRIBUTOR

1. The Promoter confirms that the start date of this scheme was the first day of January 1990, promoting widgets and mousetraps.
2. The Distributor confirms that they have read and understood the Marketing Plan and agree to be bound by the Codes of Conduct and the methods of operation as set out in this Agreement, in the current Distributors' Manual and in any official literature of the Promoter which may appear from time to time in the future.
3. The Distributor agrees that they may not have an ownership in, operational control of, or derive any benefit directly or indirectly from any second or subsequent Distributorship of the Promoter.
4. If the Promoter does not receive an annual renewal Application and the reregistration fee applicable at that time by 31 January of each year, the Distributor accepts that this Distributorship will be cancelled. The Distributor will then be required to wait a minimum of 12 months before obtaining another Distributorship with the Promoter. Any Distributor sponsored after 31 October must still reregister by 31 January immediately following but is exempt from the need to pay a reregistration fee. However, they will need to pay a reregistration fee each year thereafter.
5. No person may become a Distributor of the Promoter until they have attained 18 years of age.
6. If the spouse of the Distributor is not sponsored by the same Sponsor, then they may only be sponsored by the Distributor. The same applies to persons other than the spouse residing at the same address as the Distributor.
7. The Distributor agrees that they are a self-employed independent contractor and not an employee of the Promoter. The Distributor is solely responsible for payment of their own National Insurance contributions, VAT, Inland Revenue and other taxes and liabilities. As an independent contractor, the Distributor may not create or incur any liability of any kind in the name of the Promoter or any of its associated companies.
8. Prior to applying for an appointment as a Marketing Distributor, the Distributor must apply to HM Customs & Excise to become VAT registered and must forward a copy of the Distributor's VAT certificate to the Promoter.
9. The Distributor acknowledges that the name appearing on this application as the Sponsor, is Sponsor of the Distributor and that, if the Distributor wishes to change sponsors, the Distributor must first wait for a period of at least 12 months after resigning, before doing so.
10. The Distributor may only allow other Distributors already regis-

tered to sell products of the Promoter or participate in the Sales Programme.

11. When making retail sales, the Distributor will always provide their customer with one copy of a proper fully completed sales receipt, and within seven days act on a customer's request to cancel.

12. The Distributor may conduct their business only within the UK and such other territories as are specified at that time in the Distributors' Manual. The Distributor shall not knowingly allow any products of the Promoter to be distributed, directly or indirectly, outside the UK to any other country except as specified in the Distributors' Manual at that time.

13. The Distributor may not make any additional offers or representations to or agreements with a new or an existing Distributor in connection with this programme without the prior, written permission of an authorised officer of the Promoter.

14. Conditions for termination

15. The Distributor may terminate this contract giving written notice within 14 days of the date hereof, posted to the Head Office address of the Promoter with a copy to their Sponsor. In that event, the Distributor may require the Promoter to refund all monies paid for the registration fee and such of the business pack, any administration and sales aids and stock or samples as shall be returned to the Promoter in resaleable condition. Subsequent to 14 days from the date hereof, the Distributor may terminate on giving 14 days' notice in writing posted to the Head Office address at that time of the Promoter, with a copy to their Sponsor.

16. If this Distributorship is terminated for any reason, the Distributor cannot take up a new Distributorship with the Promoter within 12 months.

17. In the event of termination by either party, the Distributor may require the Promoter to repurchase any remaining stock at 90 per cent of the price paid by the Distributor (less any retail discounts and royalties subsequently received on that stock) provided that the stock is returned undamaged, unused and in suitable condition for resale by the Promoter as new and furthermore that the stock is received back by the Promoter from the Distributor within three weeks of the termination date, at any place and in any manner reasonably nominated by the Promoter.

18. If the Promoter withdraws from the scheme, the Promoter will refund the Distributor in full.

19. The Distributor agrees to present the programme of the Promoter in its entirety. The Distributor will make no material omissions, distortions or misrepresentations either when presenting the

opportunity to non-Distributors or when performing their respective responsibilities or obligations to their downline pursuant to the sales programme of the Promoter. Breach of this clause may result in termination of the Distributorship.

20. On termination, the Distributor will be discharged from all contractual liabilities towards the Promoters except for monies received by the Distributor from customers as an agent for the Promoter or with regard to any monies owed to the Promoter.

21. This Agreement constitutes the entire agreement between the Distributor and the Promoter or its associated companies and no other promises, offers, representations, agreements or understandings of any kind shall be binding upon the Promoter unless made in writing by an authorised officer of the Promoter.

22. In the event of the death of the Distributor, this Distributorship will pass to the legal heirs of the deceased.

While it is false economy to try to sell without samples and it is a mistake not to be a user yourself, it is possible to build a business from nothing. Although this is harder and will take you longer, at least you get the opportunity and this is why the concept has been the saviour of so many people in severe financial difficulties.

2. *Make a date to see your sponsor as soon as possible for what is called the strategy meeting.* At this meeting, your sponsor will plan with you exactly how your business is to be built. To help him or her to give you the best possible advice, you need to have ready for the meeting answers to the following very important questions:

- How much time can you give to your new business to start with?
- How much do you need to earn and by when?
- What do you want out of the business?
- What changes in your lifestyle would you like success in network marketing to bring about for you?

3. *Write out a contact list of 100 names* and have this ready for your strategy meeting. Your sponsor will show you just how this should be done. Your contact list is the most important piece of paper in your possession. It is the bedrock on which your business will grow and will keep on growing. It is so important that experienced network marketeers will simply refuse to work with a new distributor until that contact list is written. A

good sponsor will phone you the day before your strategy meeting to see if you have your list ready. If it is not, they will postpone the meeting until you have done it.

4. If you have not already been on one, *get booked into the next training session for new distributors*. The company cannot legally require you to do this if any charge is made for training but nevertheless, the more training you get, the better the chance you have of creating a successful business. Also bear in mind that, if you do not make a point of attending as many training sessions as possible, it is unlikely that your people will bother to attend.

5. *Start to teach yourself*. Ask your sponsor to recommend the best book, tape and video for you to get started with. With rare exceptions, these items are not available for sale in shops, but any company worth its salt will have book, tape and video distributors actually in the network who will sell you the training aids you need. We looked at the training LLAWR earlier, but now you should develop the '15-minutes-a-day habit', which means that you should spend at least 15 minutes every day listening to part of a tape, watching part of a video or reading a few pages of a book. This is not a lot to ask and it is amazing how much knowledge you accumulate in just 15 minutes a day. If you are not prepared to spend even this amount of time one has to ask how strong your commitment to success actually is. Just as with training sessions, if you develop this habit you will markedly increase the chances of the other distributors in your group following your example.

6. When your stock arrives, *practise, practise and practise showing and demonstrating the product*. You cannot practise too much and the better you become at showing the product, the more you will sell. You can practise with a spouse or loved one, with another new distributor, with your sponsor or with a neighbour or friend.

7. *Set your targets*. There are two major targets you need:

- How many people a day will you speak to or phone about the business?
- How much product a week you are going to retail or sell? This is going to depend largely on your personal circumstances. Some people need money immediately to pay the bills, so that is the weekly sales target they will have to set themselves just to keep going. Others have sufficient reserves to keep going for a while with no income. Even if you come into the latter category, you must still set yourself a sales

target, no matter how small it is. If you do not, you will not place enough priority on getting sales and you will be in danger of building a group with lots of people and little in the way of sales.

- Once you know what your targets are, your sponsor is in a position to show you the best way of achieving those targets.

8. *Write down your personal goals.* What rewards would success in your network marketing business bring to you? If you write down everything success will mean to you, you will find that you generate in yourself a focus, a power and hidden reserves of strength which you never knew existed and which will help you to attain what you want for yourself. There is a technique to this and, again, your sponsor will help you to make the best use of the enormous motivating power which well-written and well-implemented goals will produce.

Some people will tell you that personal goal-setting does not work. This is not true. It is the practice of it which sometimes does not work. This means that either the person has not mastered the skill of applying goals effectively or has chosen goals which they do not, deep down, want strongly enough to create the effort needed to achieve the job in hand. In other words, you must feel that the goal is worth the effort and commitment you need to achieve it.

9. *Get upline support.* This is so important that, if you do not get enough support from your sponsor, keep going upline until you get the support you do need. Remember that your uplines earn commission or royalty off your sales, so you are entitled to expect their help.

10. *Go to meetings.* Make sure you go to at least one meeting a week. If your company or the group you have joined hold opportunity meetings, remember that these are run to help you to build your business; in return, they need your support. If you are joining a good group, they will run 'sizzle' sessions, ('selling the sizzle rather than the sausage'). These are fun and you will benefit greatly by supporting them as well.

11. *Don't give up.* This is a business with great potential but the price it exacts for its best rewards is perseverance and, if you want to reach the top, dedication. I have seen so many people drop out who, had they stayed just a while longer, would have given the geometric equation time to work and so would have gone on to great things. Don't ever forget that, if you have 32 people in your business after five months, you are on course for 4,096 after a year.

12. *Don't be tempted to cut corners.* Have the patience to do it properly. In

the 50-odd-year history of network marketing, every conceivable wrinkle and short-cut has been tried. They never result in success. At best a lot of time is wasted; at worst, people drop out quite unnecessarily because they are not prepared to do the right thing.

13. *This is your business*, which means that you are responsible for your own National Insurance (NI) contributions, VAT and Inland Revenue (IR) taxes. A brief summary is given below, but you should discuss your requirements with an accountant.

If network marketing is a sideline for you, you may operate from home in a small way with no questions asked. But check the terms of your household insurance if you start a home-based business to make sure any stock in covered.

When you start in network marketing you are, in effect, running a small business. It is necessary to be organised and keep proper records, as earnings are subject to tax. It would be as well to ask an accountant how to go about it.

Keep copies of all the invoices you issue to your customers, and of those you receive from the company. Legitimate business expenses can be set against earnings before tax is calculated, and could include such items as phone calls, business stationery, postage and use of car for business purposes. You will need to have evidence of such expenditure if it is to be allowed.

The profits on your network marketing business will be added to any other personal income for tax purposes, and will be taxed at the normal rates of income tax. In the 1994/95 tax year, the first £3445 of your income is not taxed; this is known as the personal tax allowance and the amount is announced annually in the Budget. A married man living with his wife can additionally receive the married couple's allowance of £1720.

National insurance is another form of tax on earnings. For employees, it is deducted from wages by their employers. If you will be self-employed for the first time, make contact with your nearest Social Security office and ask their advice. At present (1994/95) no contributions are payable on total annual earnings below £3200. An accountant will be able to help you if you are consulting one.

Value added tax. Businesses which turn over £45,000 a year or more (1994/95) must be registered for VAT. This threshold figure is changed annually in the Budget. Registration means you have to charge your customers VAT (standard rate 17½ per cent), but you can reclaim tax charged to you by suppliers. The VAT office will specify what records must be kept. Information can be obtained from your local office of

Customs and Excise, who administer the tax.

In addition, some companies require you to become VAT registered when you reach a certain position on the marketing plan, irrespective of how low your turnover might be.

A list of useful government leaflets is given on page 93.

I hope that you can now see this business in a new light. It may be that, even if you do not feel that the idea would be of benefit to you, there are people you know for whom it could answer some small or serious questions in their lives. If so, why not lend them this book or, if you are in touch with a distributor, introduce them to each other?

Let me stress that if you do decide to come into the business, the path ahead may not be an easy one – what worthwhile part of life ever is! But if you do it right, do it with commitment and determination, learn from everyone around you and, above all, do it with patience, you will, in time, join the ranks of those for whom network marketing has led to a whole new panorama, a whole new enjoyment and a whole new quality of life.

If you are planning to become a distributor, before you choose your company and the distributor who will be sponsoring you, please read again the warning on page 7.

9

Some popular misconceptions

There are some fallacious statements commonly made about network marketing. As these are the most likely ones you will hear, it is worth covering them now.

'This is a business for salespeople'

As we saw earlier, there is not much in common between a traditionally trained salesperson and a network marketeer. Far from being a help, coming from a sales background can be a positive disadvantage because, although network marketing is itself a sales business, it is so different from the way most salespeople have been taught that they can find it difficult to grasp.

'People from a business background have an advantage'

This, too, is not borne out by the facts. Business people are often the worst sceptics where network marketing is concerned. Why should this be?

- After years of working in normal business, they often cannot believe that any business so much simpler than the ones they have become used to can actually work.
- Network marketing overturns so many of the accepted conventions of normal business that this can cause a conceptual blindness to it.
- Over the years, there has been a certain amount of unfavourable publicity, some of it caused by corruptions of the concept and some by uninformed media coverage. Business people are more likely to be aware of this and are therefore more likely to be affected by it.

The preconceptions which both business people and salespeople sometimes have can make it difficult for them to accept that network marketing is different and that there is a new skill to be learnt. This is a pity because those few who do embrace a different way of doing things find that they are in a position to turn their previous skills to advantage. It is, however, a more common sight to see them being overtaken by people who come to the concept without business or sales experience but with an open mind and a willingness to learn.

Far from business people or salespeople being the successes in the business, the American experience is that the most successful single group are women teachers – nothing to do with either business or selling!

'It is pyramid selling'

We have looked at pyramid selling properly in Chapter 6 but it is worth reiterating some points here. Pyramid selling is to network marketing what 'cowboy' builders are to those who take pride in their work, or what doctors who are struck off for malpractice are to their more caring, ethical colleagues. In just the same way that the building industry should not be judged by its cowboys or the medical profession by those who are struck off, so the proper and ethical practice of network marketing should not be judged by pyramid selling.

Pyramid selling, while never practised by more than a small minority of MLM companies, did cause great harm to some people. This was for two reasons:

- There were no set buying or selling prices, so there was nothing to stop product being sold at way over its proper, retail price. The result was that every single line of every single leg (see page 57) simply had to end with some poor distributor being caught with, perhaps, large amounts of stock at a price he could not sell. This was stopped by companies establishing proper buying and selling prices for all their products (all the ethical companies were doing this anyway).
- A distributor who got caught with stock that he could not sell had no right of compensation from the company. The law intervened and, under the Pyramid Selling Schemes Regulations 1989, Regulation 8, you can require the company to refund you 90 per cent of what you paid for the product, no matter how long you have been a distributor. This applies even to products which are discontinued by the company.

'You can only make the big money by getting in at the beginning'

This comment is true of companies with uncompetitive or poor-selling product, but you should steer clear of these anyway. But it is not true of good companies with good product.

Why is it *not* true that you need to get in early?

1. If you join a mature network, you will have proof that you are getting a saleable product and a good company.

2. People who get in early can rarely count on the level of training which a mature company will probably have developed. As we discussed, good training will make a great deal of difference to your success.
3. All mature companies can show you network marketeers who came in late but are still doing well.
4. If you have a good, long line of distributors above you (your uplines) you have all the more people you can call on to help you build your business.

People several levels above you earn royalty or commission off your sales, which makes you entitled to ask for – and expect – help from them. I have been in a start-up situation and I can tell you, from that experience, that the network marketeers who came in later than I did had an easier time – and those who came in even later had an even easier time. At the beginning, there are few people to call on for support and the systems, the training schemes, even the saleability of the product, are all untested. As the company matures, the later arrivals come into an environment where everything is proven and, most important, there will be distributors who can be held up as proof that this network does produce successful people.

Where new or start-up companies are concerned, network marketing is no different from any other form of commercial enterprise. Unproven companies in whatever market are significantly more likely to fail than established ones. However, if you do get in with a rocket, you will, as in normal business, have greater opportunities to rise faster.

'New company, or old?' is really a case of 'horses for courses'. People who enjoy the challenge of a risk will go for the new; those who want security will go for the old. Ask yourself the question, 'If I were looking for a position in my present line of work, would I prefer a new company or a well-established one?', and apply the same rule when you are looking at network marketing.

If you are someone who likes to get in at the start, take no notice of those who advocate that you should not consider any network marketing company unless it has been in business for at least two years. On this basis, no new and none of the existing ones would ever have got off the ground – and what about those people, myself included, who like to get in at the beginning?

'It must saturate'

'Doesn't the geometric equation mean that any network marketing scheme could saturate very fast? Surely, you are going to have the whole population of the UK in your business after only six months!'

It really looks as if this could happen. But network marketing defies logic and this simply does not happen in practice. Saturation, in fact, can refer to two things: saturation of distributors and saturation of product.

If we look at whether saturation of distributors is possible, this has never come even close to happening. Founded in 1959, Amway is the biggest network marketing company in both the world and the UK. Founded in 1923, Kleeneze is the most successful wholly British network marketing company and a UK household name. Yet do *you* know a distributor from *either* company – let alone both? If you do, I can assure you that you are in the minority. To prove the point that network marketing does not saturate the market, I always ask at my training sessions whether anyone present knows an Amway or a Kleeneze distributor. Rarely do more than one or two people in ten put their hands up. In fact, no network marketing company has found saturation level or even anywhere near it.

With regard to saturation of product, this, too, has never happened. Nearly every house in the UK has a television set, yet you see TV shops thriving in every high street. Most households have a car yet there are several new car showrooms in every town. Of course, many products do not sell but that is because people do not want them, not because they have them already. Where products have a market, they actually sell *more*, not less, as the market penetration increases. This may seem illogical but it is true.

10

Glossary of trade jargon

If a word is in italics, this means that it has a separate definition in this list.

Big business-builder. See *Independent distributor.*

Business-builder. See *Independent distributor.*

Downline. All the distributors sponsored into A's business after him. An example is *levels* 2 to 6 on this diagram:

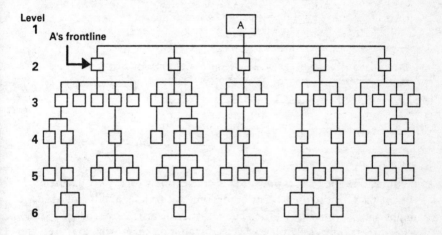

This means A is downline of his *sponsor* and also of all his *uplines.*

Frontline. The distributor is frontline to his *sponsor*, in common with everyone else sponsored by him or her:

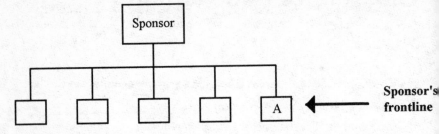

Sponsor's frontline

All the people sponsored by A will be A's frontliners, even though he may sponsor them several years apart:

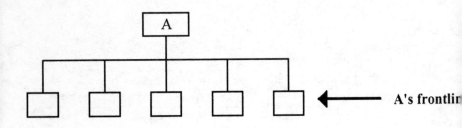

A's frontline

See also *stacking*.

Generation. The term is only used in connection with *royalty* payments. If A were paid royalty on his distributors only within a set number of *levels*, he might actually earn very little. The majority of distributors are part-time, while others only really want to get a discount on their own purchases, and so their monthly sales will be very low. Yet others will do nothing, earning A nothing.

To overcome this problem, network marketing companies no longer pay on levels. Instead they pay on generations, or a set number of 'active' distributors in each *line*. For example, on the specimen marketing plan below, the marketing manager, instead of being paid royalty on four levels, earns on the first four 'active' distributors or generations in each line – 'active' meaning that they sold above a certain minimum figure, in this example over £2,000 in that month. The difference to income is dramatic, as the following example shows:

Payment by levels	Level number	Payment by generations	Generation number
£2,000	A	£2,000	
£0	2	£0	
£400	3	£400	1
£2,000	4	£2,000	
	5	£150	
	6	£350	2
	7	£2,000	
	8	£0	
	9	£50	
	10	£700	3
	11	£2,000	
	12	£400	4

Total   £4,400   Total   £10,050

Royalty at 3% = £132   Royalty at 3% = £301.50

The generation cuts off just above the next active distributor. As you can see, the line in the example has not quite developed enough to take in the full fourth generation. You can also see that being paid on 4 generations means that, in the example of this line, A has been paid down 12 levels instead of four.

Remember that this is an example of just one line. If a distributor had a business of this size, he would be paid on many more lines.

Independent distributor (or 'distributor' – ID for short). While distributing the products of the network marketing company and operating under its guidelines, an independent distributor operates his own business entirely. Another name for an independent distributor is **network marketeer** (which can also be spelt 'marketer'). There is no clear definition as yet, but network marketeers tend to see themselves as taking the business more seriously than a 'normal' independent distributor. Network marketeers might be seen as *big business-builders*, as opposed to mere *business-builders* or *retailers*. There are three degrees of independent distributor:

Retailer. A distributor who only wants to sell product and does not want to build a business by *sponsoring*.

Business-builder. A distributor who builds a business by *sponsoring*.

Big business-builder. This is someone who is in one of the top positions of the network (see *marketing plan* and the specimen on page 90) or is aiming to reach one of them.

Leg. This is the business of each of A's *frontlines*; therefore, if A has five frontlines, he has five legs in place. This chart is exactly the same as the one under *downline* above, except that I have shaded it to show the legs:

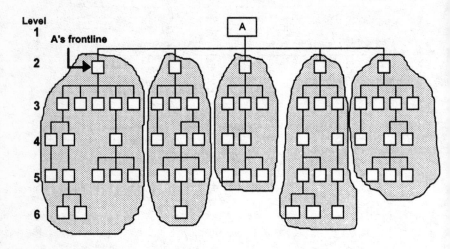

A is one of his sponsor's legs. A leg is sometimes confused with a *line*.

Level. Each level or tier of distributors. Many companies would count A as his own first level. On this definition, A's *frontline* is his second level; their frontline is A's third level, and so on. A is second level to his sponsor, as well as being frontline to him or her. The chart under *downline* above gives an example of a business with six levels. A level is often confused with a *generation*.

Line. This is often confused with leg so, to show you the difference, I have taken the *leg* (or business) of the left-hand *frontline* from the chart under *leg* and marked an example of one line in bold:

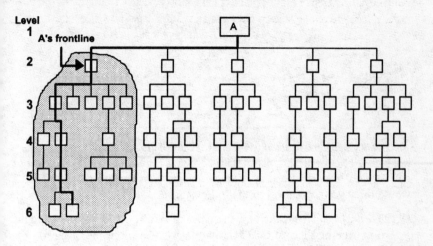

So A's business is made up of all the lines radiating out from him.

Marketing plan. In traditional business, a marketing plan is aimed at how to sell the product. In network marketing, it means the 'payment and promotion plan' – in other words, how a distributor earns his money, what bonuses he gets at each position, what positions there are on the ladder and how he qualifies for promotion to each position. I would advise you strongly not to get too involved at this stage in the detail of what the marketing plan actually means in terms of income. It is complicated and, I promise you, is not material to your decision as to whether to get involved or not (the reasons are given on page 86, where there is also an example).

The marketing plan is similar to the promotion ladder of traditional business, setting out what a person is entitled to at each stage. This might be a ladder in traditional business:

	Assistant	Supervisor	Department Manager	General Manager	Director	Managing Director
Salary	£10,000 -£12,000	£13,000 -£18,000	£19,000 -£24,000	£25,000 -£40,000	£40,000 -£60,000	£60,000 +
			Car allowance	Expenses	Expenses	Expenses
				Car	Car	Car
			Bonus	Bonus	Profit share	Profit share

The marketing plan for a network company might look as follows:

	Retail Distributor	Group Manager	Executive Distributor	Team Co-ordinator	Marketing Manager	Marketing Director
Qualification	Register	£1,000	£2,000	£3,000	£20,000	£60,000
Retail margin	20%	20%	20%	20%	20%	20%
Wholesale discount	nil	5%	10%	15%	20%	25%
Royalty	nil	nil	nil	3% on three Generations	3% on four Generations Expenses	3% on five Generations Expenses Profit share

There are huge variations in the way different companies write their market-ing plans. The marketing plan I have shown is much simpler than most but I have kept it so deliberately, so that you can understand the principle. I would draw your attention to the following:

- *Qualification.* This is the figure that a distributor, or a distributor and his group together, has to turn over in one calendar month in order to pro-mote himself. Once he achieves that qualification, he is promoted auto-matically and he keeps his promotion *even if he never hits that monthly figure again*. In other words, once a distributor is promoted he cannot be demoted and, more to the point, he keeps whatever wholesale discount that position entitles him to.
- *Royalty.* With most plans, a distributor does not earn royalties until he is part-way up the plan (in this example, until he reaches Team Co-ordina-tor). This is because he has now proved his ability to business-build and the company rewards him accordingly.

It is important to notice that, with most plans, a distributor has to achieve a certain minimum qualification each month in order to get his royalty; it is not an automatic right in the same way that his retail and wholesale discounts are.

Network marketeer. See *Independent distributor.*

Retailer. See *Independent distributor.*

Royalty. Once a distributor reaches a certain position on the *marketing plan*, he will qualify for a percentage on all the sales going through a certain number of *generations* of distributors in his group, irrespective of whether he placed the order or not. Royalty is similar to commission, although commission tends to refer to current sales whereas royalty applies to the benefit being received now as a reward for work already completed. For instance, writers and film or TV actors receive royalties now on work which has already been done and finished with; in the same way, the size of a distributor's royalty cheque now is a reflection of the amount of work put into building his business months or perhaps years previously.

Sponsor. The sponsor is the person who officially signs a new distributor into the business. Generally, this is the person who introduced the distributor to the business but not always so; see the exception under *stacking*.

Stacking Rather than being sponsored by the person who introduced you to the business, you may be put *frontline* to someone else or stacked under them. That distributor then becomes your official sponsor. There are three situations in which this might benefit you: to give you the better support of someone living closer to you than your original contact; if another distributor will have more time to spend with you to help you get your business off the ground; or because it is felt that you would be more compatible with another distributor. Conversely, if you stack someone, they are officially sponsored by the person under whom you stack them and will go into that distributor's frontline.

Upline. A's upline is every distributor from A's sponsor upwards, in a direct line of distributors going right back to one of the original distributor's *frontline* to the company:

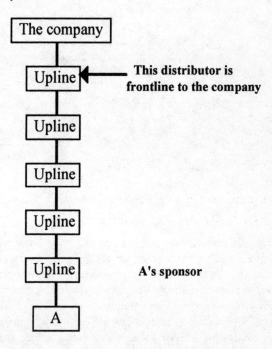

Further reading

Government publications, available free

IR 28   *Starting in Business*
IR 56/NI 39   *Employed or Self-Employed?*
IR 104   *Simple Tax Accounts*
Contact your local tax office.
CA 03   *National Insurance Contributions for Self-Employed People Class 2 and 4*
Contact your local Social Security office.

Should I be Registered for VAT?
Contact your local Customs & Excise.

Kogan Page publications

Be Your Own Boss! David Mc Mullan, 1994; contains much good advice on starting a business.
Do Your Own Bookkeeping, Max Pullen, 1988
Multi-Level Marketing, Peter Clothier, 2nd edition, 1992. Also on cassette.
Running a Home-Based Business, Diane Baker, 1994
Technology Tools for Your Home Office, Peter Chatterton, 1992

A full list is available from Kogan Page on 071-278 0433.

A selection of network marketing titles is available from Cedar Publishing on 0594 516365.

List of advertisers